Japanese Classics cookbook

The Curious Taste Of Healthy Food, Classic And Recent Delicious Japanese Recipes

Author

Candice Jordan

Unraveling the Tapestry of Taste: A Journey Through Japanese Culinary Classics

Japan is an archipelago of breathtaking scenery and a wealth of cultural traditions that has enthralled people all over the globe with its distinct fusion of the old and the new. The subtle symphony of flavours, textures, and aesthetics that has developed over ages in this fascinating country's food is its core. Japanese Classics invites you to take a gastronomic journey back in time and discover the classic dishes that have influenced this remarkable culinary heritage.

A Tapestry Entwined With Time

Washoku, a term used to describe Japanese food, is the harmonious fusion of simplicity, artistry, and nature. It honours the essence of seasonal foods by highlighting their inherent flavours and textures, and it is rooted in the Shinto principle of honouring all living things. Japanese food has changed dramatically throughout time, from the simple origins of hunter-gatherer civilisations to the exquisite grace of imperial courts.

Wet-field rice farming was first practiced during the Yayoi era (300 BCE–300 CE), and it is now a staple of the Japanese diet. The emergence of fermented foods like miso and shoyu, which would later become crucial elements of Japanese flavour profiles, coincided with the availability of rice. The development of iron tools during the Kofun era (300–538 CE) allowed for the development of more complex food preparation methods.

Asuka and Nara eras (538-794 CE) introduced Buddhism and Confucianism to China and brought forth a great deal of cultural interchange. Japanese cuisine became more refined as a result of these influences and the use of Chinese characters. Aristocratic culture reached its zenith during the Heian era (794–1185 CE), when exquisite court food had nuanced flavours and sophisticated displays.

A more sombre aesthetic was introduced throughout the Kamakura and Muromachi eras (1185–1573), which corresponded with the ascent of the samurai class. With a change in focus towards efficiency and practicality, local cuisines emerged and are still popular today. A booming merchant class and a thriving urban culture coincided with the Edo era (1603–1868 CE), which produced a gastronomic explosion. During this period, udon, soba, and tempura were developed, while sushi and kaiseki cuisine were refined.

The True Taste of Japanese Food

A few enduring basic ideas that have persisted across time are at the heart of Japanese cuisine. The savoury richness known as umami, often referred to as the fifth flavour, may be found in foods like kombu, miso, and soy sauce. Another important idea is balance, which is attained by the harmonic interaction of umami, sweet, sour, salty, and bitter flavours. Since every season brings with it a different richness of flavours and textures, respect for seasonal foods is essential.

A key component of the Japanese cuisine experience is presentation. Every little detail is taken into account, from the thoughtful placement of the dishes to the selection of cutlery. Omakase, which translates as "to leave it to the chef," is a notion that symbolises the confidence that is put in the chef's ability to provide a really unforgettable eating experience.

A Taste Adventure Is Awaiting

A celebration of this illustrious heritage, Japanese Classics provides a carefully selected assortment of traditional foods that have endured the test of time and are considered to be classics. Explore the many flavours and cooking methods that characterise Japanese cuisine with this cookbook, which has everything from sophisticated banquet dishes to traditional home-cooked meals.

You will learn the techniques for making traditional foods like ramen, tempura, sushi, and miso soup on these pages. The skill of creating dashi, the base for a lot of Japanese broths and sauces, will be covered. In order to give you a complete taste of Japanese cuisine, you will also investigate seasonal and regional specialities.

Japanese Classics is a must-have cookbook for anybody looking to introduce real Japanese flavour into their kitchen, regardless of experience level. Allow this cookbook to serve as a roadmap for your enjoyable exploration of the essence and core of Japanese cooking.

Table of Contents

Grilled salmon nigiri……………………………………………………………..10

Maki Sushi Recipe………………………………………………………………..13

Temaki Sushi Low Carb (Tuna Hand Rolls)…………………………………..18

Chirashi scattered sushi 22
Inari Sushi at Home 24
Sashimi Recipe 26
Mackerel Pressed Sushi (Saba Oshizushi)..28
Gunkan Maki Recipe | Battleship Sushi 33
Mame Gohan (Green Pea Rice)..36
Onigiri (Japanese Rice Balls) 39
Takikomi Gohan 41
Katsudon (Japanese Pork Cutlet Rice Bowl)...44
Gyudon (Japanese Beef Rice Bowl)...46
Oyakodon (Japanese Chicken & Egg Rice Bowl) Recipe...........................48
Tenmusu (Shrimp Tempura Rice Balls) 50
Kamameshi with Mushrooms 52
Omurice (Japanese Rice Omelet) 54
Easy Homemade Ramen...58
Homemade Udon Noodles from a Japanese Udon Master......................... 60
20-Minute Green Onion Sesame Soba Noodles 63
Oden (Japanese One Pot Simmered Dish)...65
Chanko Nabe 68
Dobin mushi...73

Japanese Meat and Potato Stew (Nikujaga) 76

Teriyaki Chicken 78

Tonkatsu Breaded Pork Cutlet Recipe 80

Tempura Four Ways 83

Octopus Balls (Takoyaki) Recipe 88

Yakiniku (Japanese BBQ) Sauce 91

Vegan Unagi Don (Eggplant Unagi Kabayaki) 94

Gyoza 97

Karei no Nitsuke Recipe 100

The best Ebi Fry (Japanese deep-fried shrimp) 105

Tuna Tataki 107

Miso Glazed Eggplant (Nasu Dengaku) 109

Kinpira Gobo (Japanese Burdock Stir Fry) 111

Hijiki Seaweed Salad 113

Spinach Goma Ae 115

Boiled Edamame 117

Cabbage Asazuke (Quick Pickles) 118

Hiyayakko - Japanese Cold Tofu Recipe 120

Home-made At-suage (Deep Fried Tofu) 121

Tofu Steak 124

Tofu Dengaku (Japanese Miso-Brushed Tofu) Recipe 127

Dorayaki: Japanese Sweet-Filled Pancakes 129

Anmitsu Recipe 135

Mizu Yokan Recipe 137

Mitarashi Dango (Japanese Rice Dumplings with Sweet Soy Glaze) 139

How to Make Matcha 141

Amazake 142

Ochazuke (Japanese Green Tea Over Rice) 146

How To Make Kombu Tsukudani (Simmered Kelp) 148

Cabbage Asazuke (Quick Pickles)..150

Shiso Furikake (Rice Seasoning)...152

Buta no Square simmered 154

Japanese Egg Sandwich (Tamago Sando) 156

Hamachi Kama (Yellowtail Collar)...158

Tamago Kake Gohan (Egg Over Rice)..160

Home-Style Tamagoyaki (Japanese Rolled Omelette)..162

Natto (Japanese Fermented Soybeans) 165

Tsukemono-Nukazuke rice bran pickle 168

Miso Soup with Steamed Rice...171

Grilled salmon nigiri
PREP: 40 min, TOTAL: 42 min, SERVINGS: 12

INGREDIENTS

- 200.00 gm Koshihikari sushi rice
- 20.00 gm caster sugar
- 0.60 gm salt
- 30 ml sushi seasoning
- 350 g piece sashimi-grade Atlantic salmon fillet, skin and bones removed

- 20.00 ml mirin

- 21.00 gm soy sauce

- 10.00 gm caster sugar

- Olive oil cooking spray

- Japanese-style mayonnaise, to serve

- Wasabi paste (optional), to serve

INSTRUCTION

1. Set the rice in a fine-mesh strainer. Make sure the water flows clean after rinsing it under cold water while swirling it with your hand. Make sure to drain thoroughly. In a big pot, mix the rice with 1 1/2 cups of cool water. Hide away. On a high flame, bring to a boil. Lower the temperature to medium-low. Simmer gently for 12–15 minutes, or until rice reaches tenderness and water is absorbed.

2. Take off the stove. Keep your head covered for ten minutes. Move to a wide, shallow glass or ceramic bowl.

3. To prevent rice from becoming lumpy, stir it with a spatula. Season the rice with a little salt and sugar. Add the sushi seasoning little by little while raising and stirring the rice, until the spice is well distributed and the liquid has been absorbed. Before using, let it cool to room temperature.
4. Cover a baking sheet with foil. Roll out 2 teaspoons of sushi rice at a time with wet palms into a solid rectangle (about 3 cm wide by 7 cm long) with slightly rounded corners. Before placing the rice on the tray, turn it over.
5. Lay the salmon fillets out on a cutting board. The rice should be covered with thinly sliced salmon, so cut the fish into twelve pieces about 4 cm broad by 7 cm long. Place a piece of salmon on top of the rice rectangles. Press the salmon gently into the rice. Toss in the fish and rice and repeat.

6. Light the grill to high heat. In a jug, combine the mirin, soy sauce, and sugar. Make sure the sugar dissolves by stirring. Coat the salmon with the mixture. Drizzle oil over the fish. Sear the sushi for a minute or two, moving the top 5 cm away from the heat, until the salmon is barely opaque throughout. After grilling, take off. Place on a plate and serve. Add a little mayonnaise. Toss with wasabi before serving.

Maki Sushi Recipe
PREP: 1hr 0 min, TOTAL: 1 hr 30 min, SERVINGS: 4

INGREDIENTS

- 2 cups uncooked sushi rice
- 2 tablespoons rice vinegar
- 2 tablespoons sugar
- 1 teaspoon kosher salt

- 2 teaspoons sugar
- 2 teaspoons soy sauce
- 2 teaspoons mirin
- 1 4-ounce can tuna, in water, drained
- 2 eggs
- 1 tablespoon milk
- Large pinch kosher salt
- 1 teaspoon neutral oil
- 3 carrots, peeled and julienned
- 2 tablespoons sugar
- 2 teaspoons kosher salt
- 2 tablespoons rice vinegar
- ½ bunch watercress or spinach, ends trimmed
- 4 sheets sushi nori
- To serve: soy sauce, wasabi, Spicy Mayo (optional)

INSTRUCTIONS

1. Prepare the rice as directed on the box or use our recipe for Instant Pot Rice, which calls for 2 cups sushi rice and 2 1/2 cups water. The vinegar, sugar, and salt for the rice should be heated to a boil in a small saucepan over medium heat while the rice cooks. Dissolve the sugar and salt in the cooking liquid. As the rice continues to cook, remove from the heat and let it cool slightly. After adding the

sauce, use a rice paddle to fluff, fan, and toss the freshly cooked rice. Take caution—the rice is heated. Before using, allow the rice to come to room temperature.

2. Place the sugar, soy sauce, and mirin in a small nonstick pan and heat to a simmer over medium-low heat. Add the tuna and heat, turning often with a wooden spoon, until the liquid evaporates, letting it simmer for one to two minutes until the sugar dissolves. Before using, remove off the heat and let it cool fully.

3. Gently mix the eggs, milk, and salt in a small bowl until well combined. Heat half of the neutral oil in a small nonstick skillet over medium-low heat until it shimmers and becomes glossy. After adding the egg mixture, wait 30 seconds or more, or until the edges begin to firm. Using a silicone spatula, push the edges in toward the middle of the pan, tilting the pan to enable the raw egg to spread out. Lower the heat to a minimum and place a lid on the pan. When almost all of the egg has set, let the omelet rest for one to two minutes. Then, gently turn it over, adding the last of the oil to the pan just before you do so. Once the mixture has cooled for a minute or two, take it off the heat and continue cooking, covered, until it reaches a width of around 1/2 inch.

4. Fill a basin with a few ice cubes and water to create an ice-water bath, then put it away. Quickly blanch the carrots by heating them in the boiling water for one

minute and then submerging them in the ice-water bath. Heat a small pan of water to a simmer over medium heat. After a minute or two, remove the carrots from the bath and set aside the ice-water bath for the watercress. Add the sugar, salt, and rice vinegar to a small bowl and mix it with the carrots. After 15 minutes of sitting, remove the pickling liquid and use.

5. Return the saucepan's water to a simmer over medium heat and blanch the watercress for 30 seconds until wilted. Submerge the watercress for 30 seconds, or until it wilts, then drain. Move it right away to the ice bath and wait a minute or two for it to cool. After draining the watercress, use a few paper towels to absorb any remaining water.

6. Lay down a sushi rolling mat or any other flat rollable object—we used a place mat—horizontally on a sanitized work surface. Place a layer of nori on top, shiny side down, so that the bottom edge lines up with the rolling mat's edge. A thin layer of sushi rice, approximately 1/2 inch thick, should be spread, with a 1 1/2 inch margin on the end that is farthest away from you. Set your fillings in a row, omelet, carrots, watercress, and tun, touching each other in between. Leave a 1/2-inch space of rice on the end that is closest to you. Refer to the image above. Using pressure from the mat, carefully roll the sushi away from you. Until the mat comes into

contact with the rice, use one hand to hold the filling in place. At this stage, remove the mat from the rice and continue rolling the sushi until it's entirely rolled out. Continue doing this until all of the rice has been consumed.

7. Fan out the rolls on a dish, cut them into 1/2-inch-thick slices, and serve. Accompany with Wasabi, Soy Sauce, and optional Spicy Mayo.

Temaki Sushi Low Carb (Tuna Hand Rolls)

PREP: 20 min, TOTAL: 20 min, SERVINGS: 8

INGREDIENTS

- 10 oz. canned
- 2 bulbs scallions (finely chopped)

- ¼-½ tsp garlic powder
- 3-4 tbsp roasted creamy sesame dressing
- Dash of hot sauce (optional)
- Half one whole avocado
- 2 whole persian cucumbers
- 1 medium carrot (optional)
- 4-5 pieces whole nori sheets
- 20 pieces butterhead lettuce

INSTRUCTIONS

1. To prepare tuna salad, combine all of the ingredients in a big bowl, including the tuna and, if desired, spicy sauce.

2. Create slices of avocado. Make matchstick shapes out of the carrots and cucumbers, or use a julienne peeler, like I did.

3. Separate the nori sheets into two rectangles by halving the square ones.

4. Lay a sheet of nori with its shiny side facing down. Position two butterhead lettuce leaves so that they overlap at a 45-degree angle with respect to the nori sheet's upper left corner.

5. Distribute about one spoonful of the tuna salad equally over the lettuce.

6. Start with two slices of avocado, then add carrots and cucumber. Be careful not to stuff it to the gills.

7. To make a triangle, roll the nori from the bottom left corner all the way up to the center of the top border. Maintain rolling motion until a cone is formed.

8. To assist secure the folds, dab the tip end with a few taps of water.

9. In order to keep the nori sheets crisp, eat them as soon as possible.

Chirashi scattered sushi

PREP: 10 min, TOTAL: 20 min, SERVINGS: 4

INGREDIENTS

- 325 g (1 1/2 cups) sushi rice, rinsed well
- 20.00 gm gluten-free sushi seasoning
- 2 Lebanese cucumbers, thinly sliced

- 4 radishes, thinly sliced

- 2 avocados, coarsely chopped

- Pickled ginger, to serve

- Sliced lemon, to serve

- 500 g sashimi-grade salmon, thinly sliced

- 36 cooked prawns, peeled, deveined

- Kewpie mayonnaise, to serve

- 1 green shallot, finely shredded

- 1 sheet roasted nori, finely shredded

- Micro purple shiso leaves, to serve

- Soy sauce, to serve

INSTRUCTIONS

1. Transfer rice to a saucepan over medium-high heat along with 500ml (2 cups) water. until liquid is completely absorbed. Take off the heat. Put it away for ten minutes. Stir in the sushi seasoning with a fork. Put aside to cool.

2. Distribute the sushi rice among plates or shallow serving bowls. Arrange the pickled ginger, avocado, cucumber, radish, and lemon slices on top. Add the prawns and salmon, and then pour mayo over everything. Add the microherbs, shallot, and nori on top. Accompany with soy sauce.

Inari Sushi at Home

PREP: 10 min, TOTAL: 10 min, SERVINGS: 12

INGREDIENTS

- About 1.5-2 cups Japanese sticky rice or 2.5-3 cups, cooked
- 12 Inari/Aburrage pouches juices reserved
- 1 teaspoon toasted sesame seeds

INSTRUCTIONS

1. Clean the rice well and cook it according to the package instructions.
2. Using a rice paddle, fluff the rice to release steam and get a fluffy texture.
3. Remove the inari pouches from their packaging and pour the liquid from the container or bag into a small basin.
4. Before tossing the rice with the saved inari liquid and sesame seeds, transfer it to a large mixing basin.
5. Be careful not to crush the rice as you gently mix it together.
6. Gently put a scoop of rice into each inari bag after carefully opening them in your hands. Press the rice gently into the bag using your fingers or a spoon.
7. Quickly serve by placing the inari rice side down on a platter.

Sashimi Recipe

PREP: 30 min, TOTAL: 30 min, SERVINGS: 4

INGREDIENTS

- Daikon radish about 4″ (10 cm)
- tuna Sashimi grade, block
- yellowtail Sashimi grade, fillet

- salmon Sashimi grade, block

- Shiso leaves

- Wasabi

- Soy Sauce

INSTRUCTIONS

1. Peel the daikon radish. Using a mandolin or slicer, cut thin slices. Layer the Daikon in three to four layers, then finely slice the julienne. To make it crispy, place it in a basin of water and let it sit for 15 minutes. Drain and take out the moisture.

2. Cut the tuna and yellowtail into slices that are 1/4" to 1/3" thick (6 mm to 8 mm). Thinly slice salmon at a little angle.

3. Arrange the sashimi, wasabi, shiso leaves, and radish on a platter with soy sauce for dipping.

Mackerel Pressed Sushi (Saba Oshizushi)

PREP: 40 min, TOTAL: 1 hr 20 min, SERVINGS: 2

INGREDIENTS

- 1 ½ cups uncooked Japanese short-grain white rice (2 rice cooker cups, 360 ml)
- 1 frozen marinated mackerel fillet
- 6 shiso leaves
- 4 Tbsp seasoned rice vinegar

For the Homemade Sushi Vinegar (optional):

- 4 Tbsp rice vinegar (unseasoned)

- 2 Tbsp sugar

- 1 tsp Diamond Crystal kosher salt

INSTRUCTIONS

1. Compile all of the components. Regarding the rice, please be aware that 4⅓ cups (660 g) of cooked white rice are produced from 1½ cups (300 g, 2 rice cooker cups) of uncooked Japanese short-grain rice.

How to Make Sushi Rice:

1. Measure out one and a half cups of raw Japanese short-grain white rice. Gently touch the rice with your hands in a circular manner to rinse it under cold water. After immersing the rice in water, strain the starchy water out. Repeat rinsing and washing until the water becomes clear.

2. Give the rice a 20–30 minute soak in water.

3. After fully draining the water, let it alone for ten minutes. Try your hardest to shake off the extra water if you don't have time to wait. Spoon the rice into the rice cooker's inner pot.

4. If you don't have the choice for sushi rice, pour water up to the 2 cup mark for ordinary white rice (or slightly less than 2 cups for sushi rice) and begin cooking. You may cook rice in the Instant saucepan or in a saucepan on the stove by following my instructions, but if you don't have one, just prepare 360 ml of water (we need less water than ordinary rice since you will season the rice after it's cooked).

5. Use a rice scooper or paddle to fluff the cooked rice. Soak a big bowl or a sushi oke/hangiri (a circular wooden tub with a flat bottom) in water to prevent the rice from sticking. Distribute the cooked rice equally among the sushi oke to hasten its cooling.

6. Add 4 tablespoons of seasoned rice vinegar (also known as sushi vinegar) or homemade rice vinegar (I used Kikkoman® Seasoned Rice Vinegar) to the heated rice. (To prepare your own homemade sushi vinegar, put 4 tablespoons of unseasoned rice vinegar, 2 tablespoons sugar, and 1 teaspoon of Diamond Crystal kosher salt in a vessel that fits in the microwave. Heat for 1 minute, or until the sugar dissolves. Add it to the heated rice after letting it cool. To suit your taste, add more or less. Instead of mixing the rice, use a rice paddle to slice the grain at a 45-degree angle. To keep the rice shining and from becoming mushy in the meanwhile, use a fan to chill it.

7. Turn the rice gently in between each slice. Continue doing this until the rice has cooled. Until it's time to use it, cover the rice with a moist cloth or paper towel.

To Prepare the Mackerel:

1. After defrosting, open the packaging of one fillet of marinated mackerel (shime saba). Slice the slab lengthwise in half.
2. Starting from the long edge you just cut, butterfly the fillet. To see my process, please refer to the video lesson up above. Turn the other part over as well.
3. Place the mackerel fillets on a ceramic plate and, if desired, lightly sear them with a cooking torch to produce a delicious charred taste.

4. Techniques for Pressed Sushi:

5. To stop the rice from sticking, wet your hands with the vinegar water.

6. Place the bottom base and sides of the oshibako (sushi press) mold into place so that the top may be opened. Before adding rice, moisten it with vinegar water to prevent it from sticking.

7. Lay the mackerel fillet skin side down on the bottom. Remove any extra fillet and plug any holes that may appear when the fillet exceeds the size of the container.

8. Next, place six shiso leaves on the mackerel.

9. Layer the sushi rice in a crosswise fashion. Toss the rice into the corners with your fingers, being sure to distribute it evenly.

10. Fill the mold up to the very edge, then top it up with more rice if needed.

11. Set the top half of the mold on top of the rice and firmly push down with it.

12. Once again, use your entire weight to firmly push down on the mold after turning it 180 degrees.

13. To switch positions inside the mold, turn it upside down. Carefully lower the mold's sidewall.

14. Take the upper part off. Cut the fish free from the top piece with a knife if it becomes trapped. Raise the base by pushing it up through the sidewall.

15. Now the bottom portion has the finished oshizushi. Use a knife to separate it from the base.

16. After halving the oshizushi lengthwise, cut each half into thirds. Place on a platter and top with pickled ginger for garnish. For an additional mackerel fillet, you may repeat the process. Prepare the mold for the second batch by cleaning it and moistening it. Another option is to use plastic wrap so you don't have to clean it every time.

17. Sushi Rice Leftovers: What to Do?

18. For a fast sushi fix, try making Temari Sushi or Hand Roll Sushi. The sushi rice may also be frozen for up to a month.

Gunkan Maki Recipe | Battleship Sushi

PREP: 10 min, TOTAL: 15 min, SERVINGS: 6

INGREDIENTS

- ½ cup Japanese rice
- 1 tbsp rice vinegar
- ½ tbsp white sugar
- ¼ tsp salt

- 6 strips nori seaweed

- 6 tbsp salmon roe

INSTRUCTIONS

To make rice:

1. Thoroughly wash and rinse short grains. Add ¾ cup of water to ½ cup of rinsed rice.

2. Set the rice cooker to cook.

3. Let it cool for 5–10 minutes before adding your rice vinegar, sugar, and salt combination or sushi vinegar.

4. Use a spatula to mix the cooked grains. Avoid mashing and crushing grains. Let it cool more.

How are gunkan maki wrapped?

1. Take 20g of rice, or about 1.5 tablespoons, and put it in the palm of your hand after wetting your palms with water. Close your hand gently to mold the granules. Press down firmly and mold the form with your middle and index fingers.

2. Set it down and wrap nori strips over the edges.

3. The ends of the nori may be sealed together to create a "battleship" by using water or a grain of rice as adhesive.

4. Using a spoon, carefully add your preferred toppings to the gunkan maki.

Mame Gohan (Green Pea Rice)

PREP: 10 min, TOTAL: 1 hr 10 min, SERVINGS: 4

INGREDIENTS

- ⅔ cup green peas
- ½ tsp Diamond Crystal kosher salt
- 1 ½ cups uncooked Japanese short-grain white rice
- ½ Tbsp sake
- ½ tsp Diamond Crystal kosher salt
- 1 piece kombu (2 x 2 inches, 5 x 5 cm per piece)

INSTRUCTIONS

1. Combine all parts. Uncooked Japanese short-grain rice yields 4⅓ cups (660 g) of cooked white rice for steamed rice, enough for 4 servings of rice bowls. Discover how to prepare short-grain rice using a donabe, Instant saucepan, saucepan on the stove, or rice cooker. Rinse ⅔ cup green peas quickly. Rinse 1½ cups of uncooked Japanese short-grain white rice and make sure it's fully drained (for instructions on how to rinse rice, go here).

2. Add ½ tsp Diamond Crystal kosher salt to 2 cups (480 ml) boiling water in a medium pot.

3. Once the green peas are firm yet tender—you can test this by eating one—add them and simmer for a further four minutes. Take the peas from the stove and allow them to cool in the cooking liquid. The peas won't wrinkle as a result of this.

4. Set aside 1 cup (240 ml) of the cooking liquid when the peas have cooled.

5. Place the well-drained rice in the inner pot of a rice cooker. Transfer the cooking liquid that was set aside. Fill the 2-cup line of the rice cooker with extra water. Mix well after adding ½ Tbsp sake and ½ tsp Diamond Crystal kosher salt. After adding one piece of dried kelp, or kombu, to the rice, simmer it. I normally add additional water to accommodate my family's preferences, as you can see in the photograph where the water is at the 2½-cup line.

6. After cooking the rice, remove the kombu.

7. Next, include the peas and gently mix them with the steaming rice. The residual heat will cause the peas to change color. And thus, it's not a good idea to leave the rice in the rice cooker for more than two hours. There are two options available to you: One of two options is to either 1) move the rice to an airtight container and preserve it, or 2) add green peas to the quantity you need.

To Keep:

1. Seal the leftover rice in airtight containers to keep moisture. Let the containers cool completely before freezing (see my instructions)

Onigiri (Japanese Rice Balls)

PREP: 20 min, TOTAL: 1 hr 0 min, SERVINGS: 4

INGREDIENTS

- 4 cups uncooked short-grain white rice
- 5.5 cups water, divided
- 0.25 teaspoon salt
- 0.25 cup bonito shavings
- 2 sheets nori (dry seaweed), cut into 1/2-inch strips
- 2 tablespoons sesame seeds

INSTRUCTIONS

1. Clear the water from the rice using a mesh strainer. In a saucepan, combine 4 1/2 cups of water with the rinsed rice. Stir occasionally while you boil on high. Cover and simmer the rice on low for 15–20 minutes until all the water is absorbed. After 15 minutes of resting, the rice will continue to steam and soften. After cooking, let the rice cool.

2. To prepare your hands for handling rice, mix the salt and remaining 1 cup of water in a small basin. Split the cooked rice into eight equal servings. To make one serving of onigiri, use one cup of rice.

3. Partition the rice into two equal halves. Indent the rice with a spoon and fill it with a generous amount of bonito flakes. Press gently to seal the contents within the rice ball, then cover with the remaining rice. Shape the rice into a triangle by gently pressing it; wrap it in a nori strip and sprinkle sesame seeds on top. Continue with the rest of the rice.

Takikomi Gohan

PREP: 10 min, TOTAL: 40 min, SERVINGS: 4

INGREDIENTS

- 2 cups water
- 10 grams dried shiitake mushrooms
- 310 grams Japanese short-grain rice

- 1 tablespoon vegetable oil
- 50 grams carrots
- 50 grams maitake mushrooms
- 50 grams burdock
- 1 sheet aburaage
- ¼ cup sake
- 2 tablespoons soy sauce
- 2 teaspoons evaporated cane sugar
- 1 teaspoon konbu cha
- Mitsuba

INSTRUCTIONS

1. Before using, give the shiitake mushrooms a good soak in 2 cups of water.
2. After rehydrating the mushrooms, remove excess moisture by pressing on them and cut off and throw away the stems. Remove the mushrooms and their soaking liquid from the heat and finely slice the caps.
3. Make sure the water flows clean before washing the rice. After rinsing, transfer to a Dutch oven or other deep pot with a heavy bottom.
4. Add the rice to the saucepan with 1 3/4 cups of shiitake stock. Soak it for a minimum of half an hour.
5. In a skillet set over medium-high heat, combine the shiitake, carrots, maitake, burdock, and aburaage with the vegetable oil. Reduce the amount of the components by halves while stirring.

6. With stirring, add sugar, soy sauce, sake, and konbu cha. Stir occasionally as the liquid almost evaporates.

7. Put the rice in the pot with the vegetables and mushrooms, cover, and boil over high heat.

8. If steam escapes from the top, set a 13 minute timer and low heat.

9. Remove the pot from the heat and let the rice steam for 10 minutes after the timer goes off.

10. After the timer goes off, uncover the container and gently incorporate the Takikomi Gohan into the veggies and mushrooms.

11. Before serving, top with onions, mitsuba, or sesame seeds.

Katsudon (Japanese Pork Cutlet Rice Bowl)

PREP: 5 min, TOTAL: 20 min, SERVINGS: 4

INGREDIENTS

- 2 cups dashi or chicken broth
- 2 medium onions, sliced
- 4 tablespoons low sodium soy sauce
- 4 tablespoons mirin

- 4 teaspoons sugar

- 4 eggs, lightly beaten

- 4 tonkatsu (Japanese pork cutlet), sliced

- 4 cups cooked short grain rice

- 2 green onions, sliced

INSTRUCTIONS

1. Place the onions, soy sauce, mirin, sugar, and dashi in a medium saucepan. Bring to a boil and cook until the onions are soft.
2. Cover the onions and broth with the eggs, place the pork on top, and leave for one to two minutes, or until the eggs are just set.
3. After dividing the rice among four dishes, top with the egg and pork combination and garnish with the green onions, and serve!

Gyudon (Japanese Beef Rice Bowl)

PREP: 1hr 0 min, TOTAL: 1 hr 30 min, SERVINGS: 4

INGREDIENTS

- 400 g (14 oz) Wagyu rump steak (chill in the freezer for one hour)
- 2 cups Japanese short-grain rice
- 1 tbsp vegetable oil
- 2 onions, thinly sliced

- 2 soft boiled eggs, halved
- 4 tbsp Japanese pickled ginger, to serve
- 4 tbsp finely sliced spring onion (scallions)
- Stir-fry sauce:
- 4 tbsp mirin
- 2 tbsp soy sauce
- 1 tsp dark soy sauce
- 2 tbsp brown sugar

INSTRUCTIONS

1. Freeze the steak until firm, 60–90 minutes.

2. Run some water over the rice three or four times to wash and rinse it. Simmer 2¼ cups of water with the rice in a rice cooker. A pot over medium heat should boil. Cover and simmer on low for 12-13 minutes until the rice is cooked and the water is absorbed. Turn off the heat and let the rice steam for 10 minutes with the lid on before serving.

3. Mix sauce ingredients in a small dish. Set aside.

4. Thinly slice the meat using a sharp knife.

5. Divide rice among bowls.

6. Fry now! Heat oil in a big pan on high. Add onions and stir-fry for 1 minute. Add meat. After a minute of coloring on the first side, throw the meat in the pan. To rapidly heat and bubble the sauce, drizzle it about the pan. Mix meat with sauce. Place the meat to one side of the pan so the sauce is directly over the heat source.

Bubble and thicken the sauce for 1-2 minutes. Throw the steak back in the sauce. Spoon meat over rice in each bowl after removing from heat. Add half an egg, pickled ginger, and spring onion and serve.

Oyakodon (Japanese Chicken & Egg Rice Bowl) Recipe

PREP: 2 min, TOTAL: 10 min, SERVINGS: 1

INGREDIENTS

- 1 chicken thigh
- ½ of medium size onion
- 2 Tbs. mitsuba, flat leaf parsley, cilantro, chive or green onion
- 2 Tbs. soy sauce
- 1 Tbs. mirin
- 1 Tbs. sake (rice wine)
- 1 Tbs. sugar
- ½ cup dashi stock
- 2 eggs
- 1 cup warm cooked rice

INSTRUCTIONS

1. Roughly chop the mitsuba (or other herb of choice) and leave aside. Cut the chicken thighs into bite-sized pieces. Slice the onion into pieces that are ¼ to ½ inch broad.

2. Put the soy sauce, mirin, sake, sugar, and dashi stock in a mixing bowl and whisk to dissolve the sugar. Put aside. Break open the eggs into a separate basin and gently mash the white and yolk, being careful not to stir or overmix.

3. Transfer sauce to an 8-inch donburi-nabe pan and heat it to a boil over high heat. Spread the chicken and onion pieces equally, then cover. Simmer for 7 to 8 minutes. To ensure consistent cooking, flip the chicken and onion after half the cooking time.

4. Evenly pour eggs over the surface, cover, and cook for 10 to 30 seconds, or until done to your liking. Top with a generous pinch of mitsuba and serve with warm cooked rice. Have fun

Tenmusu (Shrimp Tempura Rice Balls)

PREP: 15 min, TOTAL: 1 hr 15 min, SERVINGS: 8

INGREDIENTS

- 200 g/7 oz Nishiki sushi rice
- 8 tail-on shrimps, peeled and deveined
- 3 tbsp Kikkoman regular soy sauce
- 2 sheets Okada nori seaweed
- 500 ml/2 cups water
- 1 tbsp Mizkan rice vinegar
- 100 g/7 oz Showa tempura batter
- 1 tbsp sugar

INSTRUCTIONS

1. Before cooking, rinse rice under running water. Boil the water and add a bit of salt.
2. Put the sugar and rice vinegar in a bowl and stir until well combined.
3. After the rice is done cooking, remove it from the water and transfer it to a big basin. Toss in the rice vinegar and sugar mixture.
4. In a damp towel-lined wooden basin, let the rice cool.
5. Warm the oil from the vegetables in a small pot.
6. In a bowl, combine the tempura batter.
7. Roll the shrimp in the tempura batter and cook them in a skillet for a minute each side, or until they become pink.
8. To drain oil, place cooked shrimp on a paper towel-lined dish.
9. Gather a handful of rice and roll it into a ball with your hands. Make as many rice balls as you like by repeating the process.
10. Next, roll up the rice balls and wrap them in the vertically cut nori paper.
11. Once the shrimp are cooked, add them to the rice ball.
12. Garnish the Tenmusu with a little amount of soy sauce and serve.

Kamameshi with Mushrooms

PREP: 15 min, TOTAL: 35 min, SERVINGS: 4

INGREDIENTS

- 1 cup short-grain rice
- 1 ¼ cups chicken or vegetable stock
- ¼ cup soy sauce
- 8 -ounces brown beech mushrooms, roughly chopped
- 1 tablespoon toasted sesame oil
- 2 teaspoons toasted sesame seeds
- chopped green onion, for garnish

INSTRUCTIONS

1. Give the rice a good 15 minutes to soak in water.
2. Remove any excess water by draining and rinsing thoroughly.
3. Get the stock and soy sauce hot in a saucepan. Avoid boiling.
4. Set the clay pot on the stovetop with the iron inside. Turn the heat to medium-low. (A heat diffuser may be used if necessary.)
5. Put the rice and mushrooms in the pot.
6. Stir in the heated soy and stock.
7. Add a little stirring.
8. Allow to simmer for around fifteen to twenty minutes, or until the liquid has been absorbed.
9. Toss in some chopped green onions, toasted sesame seeds, and sesame oil for garnish.

Omurice (Japanese Rice Omelet)

PREP: See recipe, TOTAL: 20 min, SERVINGS: 2

INGREDIENTS

- Two tsp butter
- ½ medium onion, diced into 1/2-inch pieces, or around 3/4 cup
- 3/4 cup of one medium carrot, peeled and sliced into 1/4-inch chunks

- Two to three slices of half-inch-thick deli ham

- Two cups of cooked medium-grain rice—ideally from the previous day or slightly dry—

- Two teaspoons of ketchup plus more to pour on top

- One tsp soy sauce

- One-half cup of frozen peas

- One tablespoon of optional dashi or chicken stock

- Pepper and salt

- Safflower or canola oil, or any other neutral oil

- One teaspoon of neutral oil, such as safflower or canola.

- Four eggs

- One tsp water or dashi

- Pepper and salt

INSTRUCTIONS

1. Rice should be cooked: A big skillet should be heated over medium-high heat. Toss in the carrots and onion after adding the 1 tablespoon of butter. About 3 minutes into cooking, stir-fry the onion until it becomes translucent and slightly caramelized on the edges. Cook the ham for around 30 seconds, stirring occasionally, until it starts to color.

2. Before adding the rice, which should be broken up with a wooden spoon or long chopsticks, add the remaining 1 tablespoon of butter. Reduce heat to medium and sauté for 1–2 minutes, or until grains become glossy. Mix the soy sauce and ketchup and simmer for 30 seconds to caramelize. While peas are heating, add them and use dashi or chicken stock to deglaze the pan. Once cooked, remove from heat and add salt and pepper as desired.

3. After lightly oiling a small bowl with canola or safflower oil, compress 1 cup of rice into it to create an ideal mound on each dish. Turn it upside down onto a platter and take the bowl out. On a separate dish, repeat with the remaining rice.

4. Whip up the omelet: Put half a teaspoon of oil, or enough to coat the pan, into a small (6- or 7-inch) nonstick skillet (or a well-seasoned carbon steel omelet pan) and set it over medium-high heat. Two eggs and half a teaspoon of water should be whisked together . Add a little salt and minimal pepper.

5. Transfer the egg mixture to the pan that has been heated. Using chopsticks or a fork, whisk the eggs continually while shaking and swirling the pan over the heat. Allow to simmer, uncovered, for another 30 seconds or until little curds have formed and eggs are custardy. To release the omelet, run a butter knife or tiny spatula over its edge and smack the pan hard against the burner. To serve,

place the omelet custard side down on top of the rice. To conceal the edges of the rice, use a dry paper towel or dish towel to press them under.

6. For the second omelet, use the remaining two eggs in the same way. Before serving, garnish the omelets with a zigzag pattern of ketchup (or make a charming design if you're steady-handed).

Easy Homemade Ramen

PREP: 10 min, TOTAL: 30 min, SERVINGS: 4

INGREDIENTS

- 2 large eggs
- 1 tablespoon olive oil
- 4 cloves garlic, minced

- 1 tablespoon freshly grated ginger
- 4 cups reduced sodium chicken broth
- 4 ounces shiitake mushrooms
- 1 tablespoon reduced sodium soy sauce
- 3 (5.6-ounce) packages refrigerated Yaki-Soba, seasoning sauce packets discarded*
- 3 cups baby spinach
- 8 slices Narutomaki, optional*
- 1 carrot, grated
- 2 green onions, thinly sliced

INSTRUCTIONS

1. Boil a pot of water and add the eggs, being sure to cover them by an inch. Simmer for 1 minute after coming to a boil. After 8 to 10 minutes, take the pan from the heat and cover the eggs with a lid that fits snugly. After letting it cool, peel it and cut it in half. Drain thoroughly.
2. Toss the olive oil into a big Dutch oven or stockpot and set it over medium heat. After a minute or two of stirring, add the ginger and garlic and simmer, stirring often, until they release their aroma.
3. Whisk in the three cups of water, soy sauce, mushrooms, and chicken broth.
4. After the mixture boils, reduce heat and simmer for 10 minutes to tenderize the mushrooms. Loosen Yaki-Soba by stirring for two or three minutes before cooking.
5. Stir Narutomaki, carrot, green onions, and spinach for 2 minutes until spinach wilts.
6. Quickly top with eggs and serve.

Homemade Udon Noodles from a Japanese Udon Master

PREP: 10 min, TOTAL: 45 min, SERVINGS: 4

INGREDIENTS

- 400 g plain flour/all purpose flour bread flour works even better!
- 200 ml water iced or cold

- 1 tbsp salt

- cornstarch/cornflour

INSTRUCTIONS

1. In a bowl, combine the salt and cold water; whisk until the salt dissolves. Save 2 tablespoons for a later time.
2. A big mixing basin is the best place to put the flour. Add the salt water to the flour, reserving some for later. To make fluffy strips, combine the flour and salt water with your claw-shaped finger tips.
3. Knead in the remaining 2 tablespoons of salt water using your thumbs and palms until a rough ball forms, then set aside.
4. Press the dough into a big plastic bag after rolling it into a ball. Hop off the loom when the dough reaches a width of around 20 cm / 8 inches, and then fold it in half four times, as if you were sealing a cardboard box. Return it to its plastic wrapper and spread it out once more with your feet. This is the secret to perfectly tender udon, so be sure to repeat the process 20 or 30 times.
5. Take it out of the packaging and fold it into a clamshell. Extract as much air from the ball as you can by pressing its edges toward its center. Put in a plastic bag and seal it. Then, wrap it in a tea towel. Just take a half an hour to relax somewhere warm.
6. After removing the dough from the plastic bag, place it on a floured surface and use your palms to flatten it into a circle. Apply a generous amount of cornstarch and use a rolling pin to flatten until it is 1 cm / ½ inch thick.
7. Using a pasta maker for cutting.

8. Separate the dough into four equal portions. Roll each portion out using the pasta roller set to Size 0. Shape the dough into a rough rectangle. Finish up the first two steps using Size 0, then go on to Size 1 and repeat the process twice more.

9. The next step is to run the dough through the machine's fettuccine cutter. To prevent the noodles from sticking together, dust with more cornstarch if needed.

10. For manual cutting:

11. Roll out the dough by rolling it around the rolling pin and then rolling it over again, pushing forward four times to make it thinner. Roll twice from top to bottom, and then again from left to right, in this manner. Keep the dough's thickness at around ½ cm / ¼ inch.

12. Transfer the dough sheet to a work surface suitable for cutting. To make a rough rectangle, sprinkle on lots of cornflour and fold in half, like you would a letter.

13. Cut the dough into 3/4 inch broad pieces.

14. Separate the noodles into smaller pieces, then place them in your hands. To get rid of any extra cornflour, tap the noodles a few times on the cutting board. Tease apart the strips of noodles gently.

15. Prepare the udon noodles by:

16. Get a big saucepan of water boiling. After around 5 minutes, add the udon noodles and simmer until they are al dente.

20-Minute Green Onion Sesame Soba Noodles

PREP: 8 min, TOTAL: 20 min, SERVINGS: 7

INGREDIENTS

- 1 lb dry soba (buckwheat) noodles
- ½ cup low-sodium soy sauce
- ¼ cup rice vinegar

- ¼ cup toasted sesame oil
- ¼ tsp freshly ground black pepper
- 1 ½ Tbsp sugar
- 2 Tbsp olive oil
- 2 bunches green onions, sliced
- 10 oz frozen edamame, thawed
- 1 Tbsp sesame seeds

INSTRUCTIONS

1. Heat a large saucepan of water on high and boil. When the soba noodles are just soft, add them, mix, and simmer for 4–6 minutes. To prevent noodles from clinging to one another, drain and rinse with cold water.

2. In the meanwhile, thoroughly mix the sugar, sesame oil, soy sauce, rice vinegar, and black pepper in a dish; leave away.

3. In a big, deep pan, preheat the olive oil over medium-high heat. Once heated, add the green onions and sauté until aromatic, about 30 seconds. Add the noodles, then sprinkle the edamame and soy sauce combination on top of the noodles. Gently toss until the sauce is mostly absorbed.

4. Garnish with sesame seeds and serve at room temperature or chilled.

Oden (Japanese One Pot Simmered Dish)

PREP: 20 min, TOTAL: 1 hr 10 min, SERVINGS: 4

INGREDIENTS

- 1 small daikon
- 1 packet konnyaku
- 4 small potatoes
- 1 packet oden set
- 4 shitake mushrooms
- 4 kombu knots
- 4 Napa cabbage leaves

- 4 oz spinach

- 3 cups second dashi stock

- 2 tbsp soy sauce

- ¼ cup mirin (60ml)

- ¾ tsp salt

INSTRUCTIONS

1. The daikon should be peeled and then sliced into ½ inch thick cylinders. Give each daikon cylinder a little trim. Before cutting the konnyaku in half, make diagonal cuts into two equal halves.
2. Get a big saucepan of water boiling. Cook the potatoes, daikon, and konnyaku for two minutes. Take out using a strainer.
3. To the boiling water, add the various fish cakes from the oden set. Rinse and reserve.
4. In a casserole dish, mix together the dashi stock, soy sauce, mirin, and salt. Heat it until it boils. Onion, konnyaku, potatoes, and mushrooms should be added. Simmer for 30 minutes, stirring occasionally, over low heat.
5. While that's happening, blanch the Napa cabbage for a minute or two in boiling water. Repeat with the spinach; it should take about 30 seconds. Get every last drop of water out of the veggies by draining and squeezing them.
6. On the work area, lay out the cabbage leaves. Make four separate bundles of spinach and roll each one up neatly. Set a bundle on a cabbage leaf. Gently roll the cabbage leaves.

7. Lay out two cabbage rolls parallel to each other and insert two bamboo skewers into each roll. Make two more cabbage rolls and repeat.

8. Using the two skewers, cut the cabbage rolls in half. Cut off the corners.

9. Toss in some kombu knots, skewered cabbage rolls, and fish cakes of all kinds. Keep simmering for a further ten minutes. Turn the heat off.

10. Take it off and put it on right away.

Chanko Nabe

PREP: 20 min, TOTAL: 40 min, SERVINGS: 4

INGREDIENTS

500 g of ground pork or poultry; 2 tablespoons freshly grated ginger; 2 stocks chopped green onions

One tsp white pepper

- Two soy sauce teaspoons

- A single egg

- Sesame oil, two teaspoons

- 1.5 tablespoons of cornflour are optional.

- A cup or two to five of salted chicken broth

- Two slender ginger slices

- 2-3 grates of garlic

- Napa Cabbage

- Carrots

- The mushroom known as Shemiji

- Shiitake Mushroom

- Shiitake Mushroom

- Mix one egg, sesame oil, white pepper, chopped green onion, freshly grated ginger, and cornflour (if preferred) with the ground pork or chicken. Take a 20-minute break for it.

- In a saucepan, combine the sliced ginger, grated garlic, and chicken stock. Turn the heat up to medium-high and simmer for 10 minutes.

- Create a 1.5-tbsp chunk out of each meatball and set it aside.

- Place a lid on the soup, add all the vegetables, and boil.

- Next, add the meatballs and boil for an additional 10 to 12 minutes, or until the meatballs are cooked.

- Serve the meal on a portable hob either plain or with extra toppings like sliced pork belly, extra vegetables or shellfish.

Chanko Nabe:

Subjects:

Meatballs prepared at home:

- 500 grammes of pork or chicken meal

- In stock, two chopped green onions

- TWO TOPTS of freshly grated ginger

One tsp white pepper

- Two soy sauce teaspoons

- A single egg

- Sesame oil, two teaspoons

- 1.5 tablespoons of cornflour are optional.

Hold:

- A cup or two to five of salted chicken broth

- Two slender ginger slices

- Two to three garlic gratings

Garnishes with vegetables:

- Napa Cabbage

- Carrots

- The mushroom known as Shemiji

- Shiitake Mushroom

- Shiitake Mushroom

INSTRUCTIONS

1. Combine ground chicken or pork with one egg, sesame oil, white pepper, freshly grated ginger, chopped green onion, and cornstarch (if using). Give it a 20-minute break.

2. Place grated garlic, sliced ginger, and chicken stock in a saucepan. After putting it on medium-high heat, simmer it for ten minutes.

3. Shape each meatball into a 1.5 tbsp portion and save.

4. Add all of the veggies to the soup, cover, and heat through.

5. After that, add the meatballs and boil until the meatballs are cooked, 10 to 12 minutes more.

6. Present the dish either as is or with additional garnishes like more veggies, sliced pork belly, or seafood on a portable cooktop.

Dobin mushi

PREP: 45 min, TOTAL: 1 hr 15 min, SERVINGS: 4

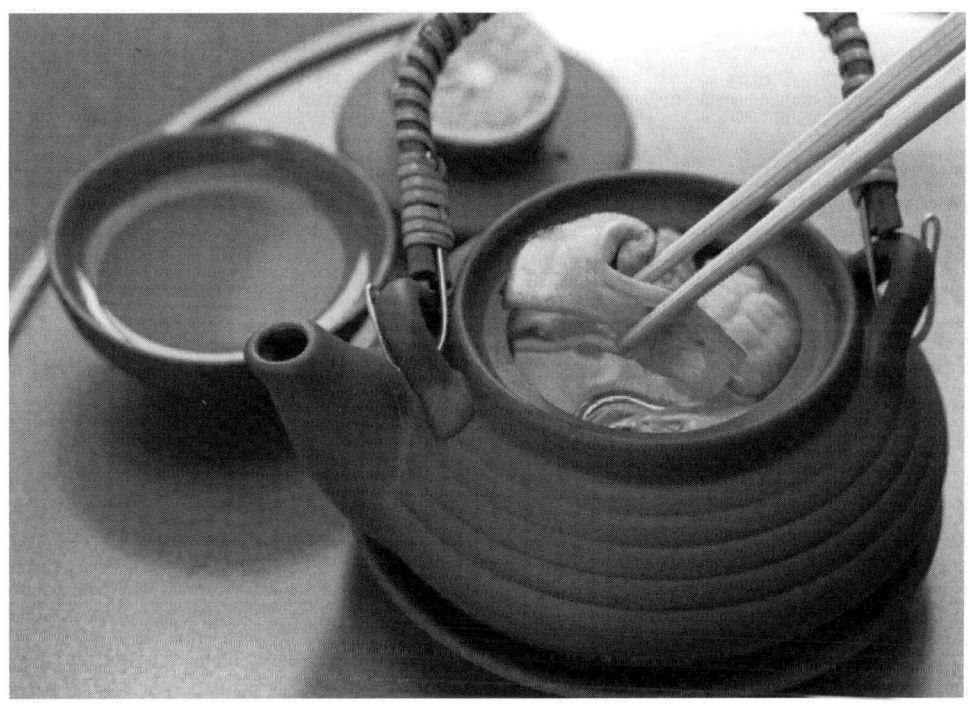

INGREDIENTS

- 1200 ml water
- 15 cm konbu (dry kelp)
- 30 g dried bonito flakes
- 1 cluster shimeji mushroom
- 4 whole prawns
- 4 chicken tenderloins
- 8 ginkgo nuts
- bunch of mizuna, finely chopped
- 800 ml dashi stock
- ½ lemon
- 5 g salt
- 5 ml light soy sauce
- 10 ml Japanese sake

INSTRUCTIONS

Over medium heat, bring the water and konbu to a simmer in a saucepan to make the dashi stock. Bring to a simmer, then remove the konbu just before it boils. After adding the bonito flakes, take the pan off the heat. Use a kitchen towel to strain the dashi stock. Instead of squeezing the bonito flakes, throw them away. To expedite the cooling process, place the dashi stock in a basin of icy water. The stock's flavor will deteriorate with time if left to cool. Quickly blanch the shimeji mushrooms after dividing them into two or three pieces. Remove the prawns' shells and veins, but save their tails. Get out of the water as soon as it boils. After de-sinewing the bird, cut it into slices. Bring to a boil and cook until the top becomes white. Use the back of a knife to crack open the ginkgo nut and remove its shell. Put the ginkgo nuts into boiling water. While the ginkgo nuts are cooking, roll them with a ladle to loosen their skin, and then peel off the thin coating. In a saucepan, combine the dashi stock. Add the sauce mixture and season to taste when it begins to boil. In a dobin teapot, combine the chicken, prawns, mushrooms, and ginkgo nuts. Transfer the dashi stock to the pan. Put the griller on top of the dobin teapot on a gas burner. Remove from the heat after the ingredients have cooked. After that, fold in the mizuna. Optional: garnish with squeezed lemon.

Japanese Meat and Potato Stew (Nikujaga)

PREP: 10 min, TOTAL: 25 min, SERVINGS: 2

INGREDIENTS

- 200 g thinly sliced beef
- 2 potatoes , cut into 3-4cm cubes
- 120 g onion (, sliced into 1cm wide)
- 60 g carrot thinly sliced into 4-5mm thick
- 100 g shirataki ((konnyaku yum noodles) cut into long strands about 10cm long
- 1 tbsp oil
- 350 ml dashi stock

- 2 tbsp cooking sake
- ½ tbsp mirin
- 2 tbsp soy sauce
- 1 tbsp sugar
- 50 g green beans

INSTRUCTIONS

1. Slice the steak into big, bite-sized pieces if each slice is huge.

2. Fill a pot with oil and turn the heat up to medium-high. Meat is sautéed, allowing the chunks to split apart.

3. After the meat becomes dark brown, add the veggies, including the shirataki, and sauté for an additional minute, making sure the oil coats every vegetable piece.

4. Include the dashi stock and heat until it boils. Using a ladle, remove the scum before adding the sake, mirin, and sugar.

5. Once boiling again, lower heat to low, mix in soy sauce, and cover with a drop lid. Potatoes should be cooked for approximately ten minutes, or when a thin bamboo skewer inserted into a potato easily comes out of it.

6. Spoon the green beans over the nikujaga in a serving dish, and serve hot.

Teriyaki Chicken

PREP: 5 min, TOTAL: 15 min, SERVINGS: 4

INGREDIENTS

- 1.3 pounds skinless boneless chicken thighs cut into 1 1/2 -inch pieces
- 1 tablespoon cooking oil
- ¼ cup low-sodium soy sauce
- 3 tablespoons light brown sugar or white granulated sugar
- 3 tablespoons cooking Sake rice wine vinegar or apple cider vinegar
- 2 tablespoons Mirin optional-white wine

- 1 tablespoon sesame oil optional, adds a wonderful flavour

- 2 teaspoons garlic minced, 2 cloves garlic

- 1 green onion sliced to garnish

- 4 cups broccoli florets lightly steamed

- 1 teaspoon cornstarch or corn flour mixed with 2 teaspoons water-if needed

INSTRUCTIONS

1. In a large pan, heat the cooking oil over medium heat. Chicken is stir-fried until it is crisp and lightly browned, stirring now and again.

2. In a small dish or container, combine the soy sauce, sugar, mirin, sake/vinegar, and sesame oil. Set aside.

3. Heat the garlic in the middle of the pan for 30 seconds until it smells. Add the sauce and stir-fry for two to three minutes, or until the sauce thickens into a gorgeous, glossy glaze.

4. Include the blanched broccoli. Serve the dish over steamed rice and garnish with pieces of green onion or shallot.

Tonkatsu Breaded Pork Cutlet Recipe

PREP: 10 min, TOTAL: 17 min, SERVINGS: 4

INGREDIENTS

Pork Cutlet:

- 4 Pork chops
- Oil vegetable or olive for frying
- all-purpose flour
- 2 eggs beaten

- Japanese Panko bread crumbs

Tonkatsu Sauce:

- ½ C worcestershire sauce
- ¼ C granulated sugar
- ¼ C soy sauce
- ¼ C Ketchup
- 1 Tbsp Dijon mustard
- ¼ tsp allspice

INSTRUCTIONS

Pork Cutlet:

1. In a large saucepan, heat a couple inches of oil over medium-high or high heat. A drop of water added should cause it to bubble vigorously.

2. Evenly pound the pork chop until it is about twice as wide and half as thick.

3. Shake off after dipping both sides in flour.

4. Next, dip both sides into the beaten eggs and let any extra to fall off.

5. Thoroughly coat both surfaces with the Panko bread crumbs.

6. After that, cook the pork cutlet in the heated oil for one to two minutes on each side. Reduce the amount of oil if it's too dark; it should be cooked thoroughly and golden.

7. To drain, place on paper towels over newspaper.

8. Chop and arrange on top of heated rice.

Tonkatsu sauce:

1. Heat the ketchup, sugar, soy sauce, and Worcestershire sauce in a saucepan.

2. Reduce the sauce by roughly 20% by bringing to a simmer and cooking.

3. Include the spices and mustard.

4. Take out and let to cool

5. Ready to eat now or store in the fridge for up to five weeks?

Tempura Four Ways

PREP: See recipe, TOTAL: 2 hr 20 min, SERVINGS: 4

INGREDIENTS

Four 7 1/2-by-5-inch pieces of kombu; two cups of packed bonito flakes (1 ounce), split; and two quarts of water (70°C/160°F).

- Two tsp of mirin

- Two tsp of soy sauce

- Two teaspoons of powdered matcha

- Two tsp finely ground sea salt

- Ten chocolate sandwich cookies with cream within.

- 0.75 cup, or around 2 3/4 ounces, powdered sugar without sifting

- Two ounces of softened cream cheese, or around 1/4 cup

- Two teaspoons softened unsalted butter

- A little pinch of kosher salt

- Two tsp melted and slightly cooled Wagyu fat

- Approximately 13 1/8 ounces (3 cups) of tempura batter mix, plus more for dredging

- Two tsp flour (rice).

- One-half tsp baking powder

- A quarter of a teaspoon of kosher salt, with enough for tempura

- Two glasses of chilled water

- Vegetable or canola oil, or any neutral cooking oil, for frying

- 4 big head-on raw unpeeled shrimp (4 ounces total); headless peeled and deveined shrimp are also an option.

- One big (4-ounce) carrot that has been peeled, julienned into pieces that are approximately 3-in length, and then collected into 1-inch-thick (1/2-ounce) bunches

- One package (3 1/2 oz) of fresh maitake mushrooms, sliced into bite-sized portions

- Four shiso leaves, moistened with paper towels

- Twelve uni pieces (3 ounces total)

- Six 4-by-4-inch nori sheets

- Garnish with lemon wedges, shredded daikon radish, and fresh ginger.

INSTRUCTIONS

1. For half an hour, simmer 2 quarts of boiling water with the kombu in a big pot. Pick kombu out and throw it away. Heat the kombu liquid until it boils, then turn off the heat. Add 1 1/2 cups of bonito flakes and mix well. Allow to sit for about 5 minutes, or until bonito flakes sink to the pan's base. Transfer the mixture to a medium-sized heatproof bowl and strain it through a fine-mesh strainer; remove and dispose of any sediments. Bring back the dashi, mirin, and soy sauce that has been filtered to the pan. Remove from the burner after it reaches a boil over medium-high heat. Combine with the remaining half cup of bonito flakes. After approximately two minutes of standing, the bonito flakes should have settled to the pan bottom. Transfer the dashi to a medium-sized heatproof dish and strain it through a fine-mesh strainer; remove and discard the sediments. Put dashi back into the pan and cover it to keep it heated. Gather the Matcha Salt: In a small bowl, combine the matcha powder with the salt. Set aside. Whip together the Oreo Cream with Wagyu Sauce:

2. Put the reserved cookie dough in a medium bowl and spoon the cream filling into it. To the cream filling, add powdered sugar, cream cheese, butter, and salt. The mixture should be creamy and smooth after two more minutes of medium-high electric mixing. Fold Wagyu fat into the mixture with a spatula. Put the mixture in a piping bag and poke a 1-inch hole. Spread half of the scraped

cookies with filling, and then cover with the other half of the cookies. Place on a baking pan and spread out evenly. Cover and freeze until hard, which should take at least 30 minutes but no more than 3 days. Beat the Eggs:

3. Melt the tempura batter mix in a medium basin with the rice flour, baking powder, and salt. Whisk to combine. Whisk in the cold water until barely mixed. Toss in a few lumps—do not overmix. Put aside.

4. Before heating the oil to 325°F, fill a big pot with oil until it is three inches deep. Separate a baking sheet with paper towels. Set aside the shrimp heads while the oil warms up. After deveining shrimp, be sure to keep their tails whole. Peel shrimp using a skewer. Flatten the shrimp by stretching them out and scoring them along their inner side (the long side that is opposite the deveined side). Get rid of the shrimp heads' outer shells and throw away the insides. Save the eyes for later use. Place shrimp in a separate bowl.

5. Coat the carrot bundles in the tempura batter mixture and then dip them into the batter. Turn the bundles of carrots into a circle by wrapping them around each other. About 2 minutes into frying in heated oil, the carrots should be a light golden color. Drain the carrot bundles on paper towels after transferring them with a slotted spoon or spider. Toss the mushrooms in the batter mixture and then roll them in the batter. Toast for about two minutes in heated oil, or until browned. Move the mushrooms to paper towels using a slotted spoon or spider. Coat the undersides of the shiso leaves with the batter mixture, and then dunk

them only in the batter. Approximately 1 minute after oil is heated, fry until crisp. Put the shiso leaves on paper towels after transferring them with a spider or slotted spoon. Heat the oil to 350 degrees Fahrenheit on medium-high on the burner.

6. Taking the cookies out of the freezer, coat them with batter mix and then dip them into batter. About 2 minutes into frying in heated oil, the food should become golden brown and crispy. Next, place on paper towels. Mix the batter and roll the shrimp and their shells in it. Float in the batter. Toast for about two minutes in heated oil, or until browned. Next, place on paper towels. On one end of each nori sheet, place two pieces of uni. To completely wrap the nori, fold the edges over it and roll it up. Coat the nori rolls with the batter mixture in two separate batches. Then, dip each roll into the batter, allowing any excess to drop back into the bowl. After about 2 minutes of frying, flip the batter using a slotted spatula once or twice to ensure even browning. Next, place on paper towels. Add kosher salt to the tempura according to your preference.

7. Add Tendashi and Matcha Salt to the tempura before serving. Top with ginger, lemon slices, and daikon.

Octopus Balls (Takoyaki) Recipe

PREP: 20 min, TOTAL: 50 min, SERVINGS: 20

INGREDIENTS

For Takoyaki Batter:

- ¼ tbsp dashi powder
- 10 oz warm water, 100 to 110 degrees F
- 2 large eggs
- 1/2 oz soy sauce

- ½ cup all purpose flour
- ½ cup rice flour
- ⅔ tbsp baking powder

For Fillings:

- vegetable oil, to grease the pan
- 3 oz octopus, cooked, cut into 1/4 inch pieces
- ⅔ tbsp pickled ginger, minced
- 2 green onion stalks, sliced thinly
- 1 ¾ tbsp tenkasu

For Toppings:

- takoyaki sauce
- aonori, dried seaweed powder
- Japanese mayonnaise, preferably Kewpie brand
- kizami, nori shreds
- bonito flakes

INSTRUCTIONS

1. Bring the water to a boil, then add the dashi powder and whisk until dissolved, being sure not to boil it beyond 110 degrees F.
2. While whisking the dashi, add the eggs and soy sauce.
3. The baking soda, rice flour, and all-purpose flour should be mixed together in a basin. Combine the dry and wet ingredients by sifting them together and whisking until smooth.

4. Set the takoyaki pan to medium heat and prepare it for use. Apply a little amount of oil to the inside of each pan curve.

5. *Be careful not to add too much batter, as it will expand, but fill each dip about 80% of the way to the top.

6. After a minute or two of cooking, you should see a little bubble forming in the batter. The fillings will remain in the centre and not sink to the bottom if you do this.

7. Make cautious not to overfill the takoyaki, but do add a little amount of each filling.

8. Once all the balls have been filled, go to the first takoyaki and release it from the sides using the takoyaki stick. This will flip the ball around three quarters of the way. Make sure the takoyaki is not entirely covered by leaving a small hole (about $\frac{1}{8}$ inch). More fried, crispy batter may be poured into this hole.

9. To make sure the batter bubbles, add additional batter to the pan and fill up the gaps. Keep cooking. Now is the moment to keep a close eye on the takoyaki and adjust the heat as needed. To prevent burning, make sure the batter cooks thoroughly.

10. When the batter starts to bubble, use the takoyaki stick to start turning the takoyaki. As you spin each takoyaki ball, use the stick to swirl the batter around the borders of each semicircle, folding it into each one as you go.

11. Gently fry the balls until they get a golden brown colour and have a crispy exterior. The interior temperature of each takoyaki should be 200 degrees Fahrenheit.

12. After removing the balls off the stick, coat them with takoyaki sauce, add aonori, squeeze on some mayonnaise, garnish with seaweed strips, and finish with bonito flakes. Serve right away.

Yakiniku (Japanese BBQ) Sauce

PREP: 5 min, TOTAL: 5 min, SERVINGS: 1

INGREDIENTS

- ¼ sweet onion (75 g; grated, with juice)
- 3 cloves garlic
- ⅛ tsp ginger (grated)
- ¼ tsp gochujang
- ¼ cup soy sauce
- 2 Tbsp sugar
- ½ Tbsp toasted white sesame seeds
- 1 tsp toasted sesame oil

INSTRUCTIONS

1. Gather all the necessary items. For those who like my 2014 recipe, I've included a comment below.
2. Half of the sweet onion should be minced. Make sure to collect every last drop of liquid.
3. Put shredded onion and juice in a mason jar or microwave-safe container. I use a garlic press to cut or crush three garlic cloves before adding them to the container.
4. First, I take half a teaspoon of grated ginger and shred it using a ceramic grater.
5. Blend the grated ginger with half a teaspoon of gochujang, half a cup of soy sauce, and two teaspoons of sugar in a jar.
6. Tossed white sesame seeds, 1/4 tbsp. Just 30–35 seconds in the microwave should be enough to dissolve the sugar in the sauce.
7. Mix well after adding a teaspoon of toasted sesame oil. Now the Yakiniku Sauce is ready to be used.

8. Serve me, I am here:

9. Serve with your preferred grilled meal, such Teppanyaki, Yakiniku, or fresh spring rolls, after dipping each portion in the sauce.

10. Reserved for the Future:

11. Do not keep it in the fridge for more than two weeks; use it up before then.

Vegan Unagi Don (Eggplant Unagi Kabayaki)

PREP: 10 min, TOTAL: 20 min, SERVINGS: 2

INGREDIENTS

- 3 Japanese eggplants OR 2 Chinese eggplant
- potato starch, for dusting
- 3 tbsp (45 mL) sake
- 3 tbsp 45 mL) mirin
- ½ tsp (2.5 g) kombu dashi powder, optional
- 3 tbsp (36 g) cane sugar

- 3 tbsp 45 mL) Japanese soy sauce
- nori (seaweed)
- 2 cups (450 g) cooked Japanese short grain rice
- sesame seeds, optional

INSTRUCTIONS

1. Slice the eggplant lengthwise. Either leave the skin on or pull it off. To prevent it from popping during cooking, drill holes into the skin if you're planning to keep it on.
2. Put the eggplants in a steamer and cook for four to five minutes, turning the steamer over halfway through.
3. Place in a covered microwave-safe dish and cook at 600 W for 1 and a half minutes. Microwave the eggplant for a further 1.5 minutes after flipping it over. Wrap the eggplant in cling wrap and cook it for the same length of time on a plate if you don't have a microwave-safe dish with a cover big enough to fit it.
4. For 30 minutes, turning halfway through, bake the eggplants at 350 degrees Fahrenheit.
5. Cut the eggplant in half lengthwise, then vertically across the center, being careful not to slice through. To open the eggplant, use your fingers. This step is optional, but it adds an eel-like appearance if you slice horizontally gently enough to leave lines on both sides without cutting too deeply.

6. Do not continue if you would rather use a one-pan technique. Combine the sake, mirin, cane sugar, and kombu dashi powder in a saucepan over medium heat. Add the soy sauce once it boils, and then turn the heat down to low. Simmer,

covered, for 5 minutes, or until reduced by half. If you want to avoid overcooking the eggplant, make the sauce separately.

7. Sprinkle a little potato starch on top. Make care to lay the eggplant flat when cooking it in a frying pan with two teaspoons of cooking oil over medium heat. Grill for two or three minutes on each side, or until a beautiful char appears.

8. Whisk in the dashi powder, mirin, sake, and mirin. Stir in the soy sauce and sugar after swirling the pan. To avoid flavor loss and scorching, soy sauce is often applied last. After another swirl, reduce heat to low and simmer for 30 to 45 seconds. Swirl the pan periodically while cooking until the eggplant becomes pink and the sauce has decreased. Before spooning the sauce over the eggplant, remove it from the heat.
9. Apply a coat of unagi sauce on one side of the fish, then turn it over and repeat. I find that doing it twice or three times gives the eggplant just the right amount of glaze.
10. Grill the eggplant until it becomes soft. Broil till "smoky" (about two to three minutes) if you don't have a torch. If you want, you may top it with sesame seeds and Japanese pepper.
11. After the nori, put a single layer of unagi on top. Next, fill a donburi or bowl with cooked rice, measuring about 1 1/2 cups. Top the rice with a good amount of seaweed and drizzle the remaining sauce on top. The seaweed will cling to the eggplant, imparting flavor and giving it an almost "skin" appearance and texture, so place the eggplant immediately on top of it. Get some and savor!

Gyoza

PREP: See recipe, TOTAL: 55 min, SERVINGS: 50

INGREDIENTS

- 1 packet 50 gyoza wrappers
- ⅛ head of cabbage
- 1 teaspoon salt
- 400 g lean ground pork or chicken
- ½ bunch garlic chives, finely chopped
- 4 dried shiitake mushrooms, soaked in hot water and finely chopped
- 1 tablespoon grated ginger
- 2 teaspoons soy sauce

- 2 teaspoons sesame oil, plus 2 teaspoons extra, for cooking
- Pinch of salt
- 2 tablespoons soy sauce
- 2 tablespoons rice vinegar
- La-Yu (Japanese chili oil), optional

INSTRUCTIONS

1. Finely chop the cabbage and season with one teaspoon of salt. Apply a light massage to it. After leaving for ten to fifteen minutes, squeeze with your palms to get rid of any moisture.
2. Add the ginger, mushrooms, soy sauce, sesame oil, minced pork, chives, cabbage, and a little pinch of salt. Mix everything well with your hands.
3. Dry your hands thoroughly; else, the wrappers will adhere. Using one hand, hold a gyoza wrapper and place one spoonful of filling in the middle of it.
4. Using cold water, brush the edge of half of the wrapping. The wrapper should be folded in half to create a semicircle. Using your fingers, pinch the open edges of the wrapper together to seal the top.

5. Put twenty to twenty-five gyoza in a large frying pan over medium-high heat with two tablespoons of sesame oil. Pour in enough water to fill the pan to the brim, place a lid on it, and cook over medium-high heat for 6-7 minutes, or until the food is cooked through and the liquid evaporates from the pan. Take off the lid and heat for a further 30 to 60 seconds to crisp the bottoms. Prepare any leftover gyoza or freeze them.

6. Combine vinegar, soy sauce, and chile oil (if desired). Serve heated gyoza with sauce for dipping.

Karei no Nitsuke Recipe

PREP: See recipe, TOTAL: 30 min, SERVINGS: 2

INGREDIENTS

- 2 pieces Karei Fish
- 100 ml Water
- 100 ml Sake
- 1 tbsp Sugar
- 2 tbsp Mirin
- 2 tbsp Soy Sauce
- 4 slices Ginger Root

- ½ Burdock Root (Gobo)
- Ginger Root (shredded)
- Kinome Leaves

INSTRUCTIONS

1. The karei fish, or righteye flounder, is a flatfish kind. Let's start by getting it ready.
2. Use a knife to scrape the fish's sides in order to remove the scales.
3. Squeeze off any excess moisture with a paper towel.
4. Before cooking the interior, make small incisions in the skin in the shape of an X.
5. To prevent undercooking, remove the egg sacks from the meat if they are big.
6. If you want to cook the fish at the right temperature, boil one litre of water and then add another third litre. About 80 °C (176 °F) will be the result of this.
7. Immerse the karei fish in the boiling water after placing it on a mesh strainer.
8. As soon as you see a small whiteness, drop it into a basin of icy water.
9. This will make it easier to peel off the remaining scales and lessen the fishy taste.

10. After that, set the egg sacks on a plate and dip them into the boiling water.

11. The karei fish should be rinsed gently. In order to prepare tasty simmered salmon, it is essential to follow these steps precisely.

12. Lastly, gently pat dry with a paper towel any surplus moisture.

13. The next step is to use diagonal cuts to chop the burdock root into 3 mm (0.1") pieces.

14. Give the root a quick washing and then strain it through a fine-mesh strainer.

15. We can start making the broth now. Sake, sugar, mirin, and soy sauce should all be mixed together in a saucepan.

16. Toss in the pieces of ginger root. Before heating the broth over medium heat, stir to incorporate.

17. Toss in the egg sacks and karei fish after it comes to a boil.

18. Prior to adding the fish, ensure that the broth has come to a boil. If there is any off flavour, this will help get rid of it.

19. The burdock root should be added next.

20. Ladle the broth over the karei fish after returning it to a boil.

21. Next, use a mesh strainer to get rid of the froth.

22. Place a sheet of parchment paper on top of the karei fish and use the bottom of a glass or pie dish to press it down.

23. While cooking, make sure the fish is completely immersed in the liquid at all times.

24. After 10 minutes of simmering, take the parchment paper and lid off.

25. Reduce heat and ladle broth over again.

26. At last, it's ready.

27. Transfer the egg sacks to a platter and turn off the heat.

28. Karei fish is delicate, so be careful while plating it.

29. Beside it, set the burdock root.

30. A ladleful of the broth should be poured over.

31. Lastly, add the shredded ginger root and kinome, which are the young leaves of the sansho pepper, as garnishes.

The best Ebi Fry (Japanese deep-fried shrimp)

PREP: 15 min, TOTAL: 20 min, SERVINGS: 2

INGREDIENTS

- 11 oz shrimp
- 1 egg yolk
- ¼ cup sparkling water very cold
- ½ cup all-purpose flour
- salt to taste
- black pepper to taste

- 1 cup Panko breadcrumbs

- 4 cups frying oil

INSTRUCTIONS

1. Begin by getting the prawns ready. Twist their head slightly to remove it, then pull hard on their legs to remove most of the shell. The very last portion of the shell should remain on the tail.

2. Use paper towels to wipe dry your shrimp after rinsing them under running water.

3. Using a knife, make three to four incisions on the shrimp's tummy. Then, gently press the incisions with your fingertips. They'll stay straight during cooking thanks to this.

4. Next, devein your shrimp by making a little cut along the back of the shrimp and removing the vein with the point of your knife.

5. To make the batter, beat the egg yolk in a mixing bowl and gradually whisk in the flour and sparkling water. After adding a dash of salt and black pepper for seasoning, have a bowl of Panko breadcrumbs ready.

6. Transfer the oil into a saucepan and bring it up to 350°F/180°C.

7. Coat every prawn (except from the tail) with batter and then panko breadcrumbs. Put them in the heated oil two at a time and fry until they are a lovely golden colour.

8. Set on a paper towel-lined plate or a wire rack to catch drips. While savouring:)

Tuna Tataki

PREP: 5 min, TOTAL: 10 min, SERVINGS: 2

INGREDIENTS

For the Ginger Ponzu Sauce:

- 1 green onion/scallion
- 1 tsp ginger
- 3 Tbsp ponzu
- 2 tsp toasted sesame oil
- 1 tsp soy sauce
- 1 tsp toasted white sesame seeds

For the Tuna:

- 2 Tbsp neutral oil

- ½ lb sashimi-grade yellowfin/ahi tuna

For the Garnish:

- ½ lemon

- Korean chili thread

INSTRUCTIONS

1. Compile every component.

2. Finely shred the ginger and save 1 tsp of grated ginger (with juice). Slicing thinly one green onion or scallion, put it aside.

3. Mix sauce ingredients in a separate bowl: 2 tsp toasted sesame oil, 3 Tbsp ponzu, 1 tsp toasted white sesame seeds, and green onions. Stow.

4. Turn on a nonstick skillet. Add two teaspoons neutral oil to the hot pan. Once the oil is heated, place ½ pound of premium yellowfin or ahi tuna in it and sear it for 30 seconds on each side.

5. After it's seared on both sides, take it off the fire and allow it to cool. Cut the tuna into chunks measuring ¼ inch (6 mm). After adding the sauce to the tuna tataki, garnish it with a quarter of a lemon and a Korean chili thread.

To Stock:

1. The leftovers may be refrigerated for a day if they are stored in an airtight container.

Miso Glazed Eggplant (Nasu Dengaku)

PREP: See recipe, TOTAL: See Recipe, SERVINGS: 2

INGREDIENTS

- 2 small eggplants
- 4 tbsp red miso paste
- 2 tbsp mirin
- 1 tbsp sugar

- 1 tbsp sake
- 2 tbsp vegetable oil
- Sesame seeds

INSTRUCTIONS

Before Beginning Get your oven ready by preheating it to 200°C. Using a bowl, thoroughly blend the miso paste, mirin, sugar, and sake. After halves the eggplants, score the flesh all over. Before you begin, line a baking sheet with aluminum foil. In the Kitchen Saute the eggplant, skin side down, in hot oil in a skillet over high heat. Before turning the eggplant over, cover the skillet and simmer for a further 5 minutes, or until the flesh is cooked through and the skin has browned. After taking the eggplants out of the pan, place them on the baking sheet. To coat the meat completely, brush it with the miso mixture. After 5 to 10 minutes, or when the miso is somewhat browned, transfer the baking sheet to the broiler. In Order to Assist Sprinkle sesame seeds over the eggplants after taking them out of the oven. While it's hot, serve and savor!

Kinpira Gobo (Japanese Burdock Stir Fry)

PREP: 5 min, TOTAL: 10 min, SERVINGS: 2

INGREDIENTS

- 1 stalk Gobo (Burdock), 150g
- ½ Carrot, 70g
- 1 Tbsp Sesame oil
- 2 Tbsp Water
- ½ Tbsp Sugar
- 1 Tbsp Mirin

- 1 Tbsp Soy sauce

- 1 Tbsp Toasted sesame seeds, for garnish

INSTRUCTIONS

1. Prepare the ingredients: Use running water to give the gobo a good cleaning to get rid of any dirt or debris. Peel the gobo's outer skin using a vegetable peeler or the back of a knife. Slice the gobo thinly, then soak it in water. Slice the carrot into slender segments.

2. Stir fry: Add the sesame oil to a frying pan that has been heated to medium heat. Stir-fry the carrots and gobo for a few minutes after adding them.

3. Braise: Till tender, add water and braise.

4. Season: Stir-fry for a few minutes after adding the sugar, mirin, and soy sauce.

5. Present: Arrange the kinpira gobo onto a platter and top with toasted sesame seeds for decoration.

Hijiki Seaweed Salad

PREP: 10 min, TOTAL: 20 min, SERVINGS: 4

INGREDIENTS

- 20 g (0.7oz) dried hijiki
- 2 aburaage
- 80 g (2.8oz) carrot
- 40 g (1.4oz) frozen edamame beans
- 2 tbsp sesame oil

- 150 ml (2.7oz) dashi stock

- 2 tbsp soy sauce

- 1.5 tbsp sugar

- 1 tbsp sake

INSTRUCTIONS

1. Use a strainer to drain the rehydrated hijiki, then rinse several times. Empty.

2. To get rid of extra oil, pour two cups of boiling water over the absorbage and press off the surplus water. Each abraage should be sliced in half lengthwise, then into transverse strips 5 mm (3/16") wide.

3. After a few minutes of boiling, strain frozen edamame.

4. Fill a sauce pan with sesame oil and turn the heat up to high. Stir in the carrot and cook for 30 seconds.

5. After that, add the hijiki and cook it for 30 to 1 minute. For a further thirty seconds, add the aubergine and sauté.

6. Include the flavoring components and stir. Once the majority of the liquid has evaporated, After 7 or 8 minutes turn the heat down to medium and continue cooking. During cooking, toss the saucepan a few times to ensure that the ingredients are equally coated with sauce.

7. Add the edamame and stir; remove from the heat.

8. You may serve them in separate little bowls or in a big shared dish.

Spinach Goma Ae

PREP: 7 min, TOTAL: 10 min, SERVINGS: 2

- 3 tablespoons toasted sesame seeds
- 1 teaspoon evaporated cane sugar
- 1 ½ teaspoons soy sauce

INSTRUCTIONS

1. Place a big pot of water on the burner and heat it until it begins to boil.

2. Use a big basin of water to thoroughly wash the spinach. Particular care should be paid to the areas where the stems and roots converge, since these clefts often collect a lot of silt.

3. Using a food processor, coffee grinder (clean), or mortar and pestle, ground the sesame seeds. It ought to look like wet sand.

4. Combine the ground sesame seeds with the sugar and soy sauce, stirring to blend.

5. Place the spinach, roots and stems first, into the boiling water. Once the spinach is completely immersed, return the water to a rolling boil.

6. To quickly chill the spinach, strain it once the water reaches a boil and rinse it several times under cold water.

7. With the root ends facing up, remove the spinach from the water so that all of the leaves line up. After folding the spinach in half, squeeze off any extra liquid. The spinach shouldn't be very dry, but it also shouldn't be mushy either.

8. Lay out the squeezed spinach on a chopping board and slice it into lengths of 1 1/2 inches.

9. Combine the sesame seeds and spinach and toss until the seeds are uniformly distributed. After serving, top with more sesame seeds.

Boiled Edamame

PREP: See recipe, TOTAL: See Recipe, SERVINGS: See Recipe

INGREDIENTS

- 3 quarts water
- 1 teaspoon salt
- 2 pounds frozen soybeans in pods

INSTRUCTIONS

Heat about 3 quarts of water and 1 teaspoon of salt to a boil in a 5- to 6-quart saucepan over high heat. Add two pounds of frozen soybeans in their pods, and simmer for approximately five minutes, or until the beans within are soft enough to bite through. Once you've drained, add more salt to taste. Heat and serve, or cover and refrigerate for up to 4 hours.

Cabbage Asazuke (Quick Pickles)

PREP: 5 min, TOTAL: 5 min, SERVINGS: 10

INGREDIENTS

- 560 grams napa cabbage
- 90 grams carrots

- 30 grams scallions

- 5 grams ginger

- 20 grams salt

- 2-3 chili peppers

- 5 grams konbu

INSTRUCTIONS

1. Weigh the veggies if you are using a different quantity, and then multiply that amount by .3. This will indicate how much salt to add. For instance, we're using 685 grams of veggies in total for this meal, and 20 grams of salt is equal to 3% of 685 grams.

2. Combine all the ingredients and place them into a large zippered bag.

3. Seal the bag after eliminating any remaining air. Place the sack inside one tray and cover it with a smaller tray that has cans weighted on it.

4. When the cabbage is transparent and has released a lot of liquid, the asazuke is ready to consume.

Hiyayakko - Japanese Cold Tofu Recipe

PREP: 5 min, TOTAL: 5 min, SERVINGS: 1

INGREDIENTS

- 200 g silken tofu cut to square

- 2 tbsp soy sauce sub 1 tbsp mentsuyu and 1 tbsp dashi stock

- 1 tsp ginger grated and heaped, sub myoga

- 1 spring onion

- 2 tbsp bonito flakes

- ½ tsp wasabi

INSTRUCTIONS

1. Gently transfer the silken tofu to a small plate and cover with the soy sauce.

2. Add your preferred garnishes on top. We suggest wasabi, ginger, spring onions, and bonito flakes. See the notes below for more topping ideas!

3. Press your chopsticks together to cut the tofu. Cut into little pieces and savor!

Home-made At-suage (Deep Fried Tofu)

PREP: 20 min, TOTAL: 25 min, SERVINGS: 2

INGREDIENTS

- 300 g/10.6oz fresh tofu
- Oil to deep fry
- Finely chopped shallots/scallions
- Grated ginger

INSTRUCTIONS

1. Cut the tofu in half lengthwise. It should provide two blocks, each approximately 2-2.5 cm/1¾-1" thick (note 3).

2. Arrange the tofu pieces on a chopping board covered with a fresh kitchen towel or paper. set another kitchen towel or paper over the tofu pieces, and then set an upside-down flat plate or a tray with a little weight on top of it.

3. To tilt and position the cutting board so that the extra water drips into the sink, place something below one end of the board. Give it ten to fifteen minutes.

4. Add oil to a saucepan or frying pan and bring the temperature up to 175C/347F. At the very least, the oil must be 3–4 cm (1¼–1½").

5. Using kitchen paper to blot dry a tofu slice, set it on a flat sieve spoon or a metal spatula with a slot, and carefully slide it into the oil. Because the tofu includes water, a lot of bubbles may rise, but they will eventually settle.

6. Cook the tofu for 4–5 minutes, or until the exterior is firm and gently browned. Utilizing the spatula or sieve spoon, flip it over halfway.

7. To absorb extra oil, move the tofu to a plate covered with kitchen paper using the spatula or sieve spoon.

8. Slit the in half along the length. After that, split it in half crosswise to create eight little blocks.

9. Put the at-suage on a plate and garnish with ginger and shallots. Warm it up and serve it with a side of soy sauce.

10. To consume, drizzle the at-suage and garnishes with the soy sauce.

Tofu Steak

PREP: 30 min, TOTAL: 45 min, SERVINGS: 4

INGREDIENTS

Tofu Steaks:

- 24 ounces Extra Firm Tofu (680g)
- ½ Tbsp Sesame Oil For Frying

Marinade Sauce:

- 1 Tbsp Sesame Oil
- 2 Tbsp Soy Sauce
- 1 Tbsp Tomato Paste

- 2 Tbsp Maple Syrup

- 1 Clove Garlic Crushed

- ½ tsp Liquid Smoke

- ½ tsp Garlic Powder

- ½ tsp Onion Powder

- ¼ tsp Salt

- ¼ tsp Ground Black Pepper

INSTRUCTIONS

1. press the tofu. Press the tofu for a duration of thirty minutes. Use a tofu press if possible, but if not, set the tofu on a plate, top it with another plate, and then pile heavy objects like pots or books on top of that.

2. Get the marinating sauce ready. Add sesame oil, soy sauce, tomato paste, maple syrup, smashed garlic, liquid smoke, onion powder, garlic powder, salt, and powdered black pepper to a measuring jug and stir until well combined while the tofu is pressing.

3. Season the steaks of tofu. Slice the tofu into four rectangular steaks after the pressing process is complete. After putting the steaks on a shallow tray, cover them completely with marinating sauce, and let them sit for 15 minutes.

4. Turn the heat to medium in a grill pan. Apply some sesame oil to it while it's heated.

5. Sear the steaks of tofu. Cook the two tofu steaks for three minutes after adding them to the hot grill pan. When they initially enter, they should adhere to the pan; this is OK. They ought should come out of the pan easily after three minutes. After

three minutes, turn them over and cook the other side. At this point, their grill lines need to be nice and straight.

6. Apply marinade sauce on top. Once the tofu steaks are done, take them out of the pan by brushing them on both sides with some of the remaining marinade sauce.

7. Continue with the next two tofu steaks.

8. Top with vegan peppercorn sauce and serve with vegetables, salad, or chips.

Tofu Dengaku (Japanese Miso-Brushed Tofu) Recipe

PREP: 15 min, TOTAL: 50 min, SERVINGS: 3

INGREDIENTS

- One block of firm tofu
- ⅓ cup of a miso of your choice, preferably a combination of white and red
- 2 eggs yolks
- 2 tablespoons sake
- 2 tablespoons mirin
- 2 tablespoons sugar
- 3 tablespoons dashi, or water
- Toppings (optional):

- Sesame seeds

- Grated lemon or yuzu rind

- Fresh ginger juice

INSTRUCTIONS

1. To prepare the miso dressing: Place a bowl over simmering water, or, if you have one, use a double boiler. Add the miso, egg yolks, sake, mirin, and sugar to the bowl. Add another tablespoon of sugar in favor of mirin, a sort of sweet sake used in cooking, if you can't locate any.

2. Gradually pour the dashi over the water that is simmering. Stir until thickened, then taste and adjust spices as necessary. The sauce will lean more toward the sweet or salty side depending on the kind of miso you've selected. If desired, add one of the toppings just before serving.

3. To prepare the tofu, take it out of the package and place it on a cutting board in a block form. Use a fresh tea towel to wrap the tofu. If you have a drop cover, weigh down the tofu block with it and anything suitably heavy.

4. Divide the tofu into 2-inch pieces. After skewering each piece, grill it over a hot charcoal fire on both sides, until the tofu is well roasted and the surface is browned. As an alternative, place the tofu in a shallow pan and bake it under the broiler for a few minutes.

5. Take it off the burner and drench one side heavily with miso sauce. If desired, top with garnishes like sesame seeds. For one or two minutes, or until the topping is browned, grill or broil the miso-covered side. Serve right away.

Dorayaki: Japanese Sweet-Filled Pancakes

PREP: 15 min, TOTAL: 30 min, SERVINGS: 2

INGREDIENTS

- 2 large eggs
- ⅔ cup sugar
- ½ teaspoon baking soda
- 3 tablespoons water
- 1 cup all-purpose flour
- vegetable oil
- ¾ pound anko

INSTRUCTIONS

1. Assemble the components.

2. combine the eggs and sugar and mix well.

3. Use water to dissolve baking soda.

4. Stir the egg mixture with water.

5. Gradually stir sifted flour into egg mixture.

6. Lightly oil and heat a pan or hot plate.

7. Using a spoon, scoop out some batter and use it to form a little pancake that is between three and four inches across.

8. When bubbles form on the surface, flip it over.

9. Do this step again for every pancake.

10. Allow the pancakes to cool.

11. Create pancake pairs and place a dollop of anko sweet beans in between.

Taiyaki

PREP: 10 min, TOTAL: 20 min, SERVINGS: 4

INGREDIENTS

- 2 teaspoons vegetable oil
- 75 grams cake flour
- 25 grams shiratamako
- ¼ teaspoon baking powder
- ¼ teaspoon baking soda
- ½ cup milk
- 2 tablespoons cultured unsalted butter
- 1 tablespoon honey
- ½ teaspoon vanilla extract

- 120 grams anko

INSTRUCTIONS

1. Gather two tablespoons of vegetable oil and roll up a piece of paper towel tightly. Before anything else, make sure the oil soaks into the paper towel completely.
2. 75 grammes of cake flour, 25 grammes of shiratamako, 1/4 teaspoon of baking soda, and 1/4 teaspoon of baking powder should all be sifted into a sieve set over a medium-sized bowl.
3. Preheat a microwave-safe bowl on high for 50 seconds, stirring occasionally, until the milk, cultured unsalted butter, honey, and vanilla essence are all combined. Combine the ingredients and whisk until the butter has melted.
4. For the Taiyaki batter, mix the wet and dry ingredients; whisk until well incorporated and lump-free.
5. On the lowest heat setting, bring the Taiyaki pan to a temperature of about 285°F, or 140°C, on both sides.

6. Grease the mould gently using the paper towel saturated with oil. No oil bubbles should form on the pan's surface.

7. Spoon one spoonful of batter into each corner of the mould. Pour batter into the mold's cavities and up its sides using a pastry brush that can withstand high temperatures.

8. After the batter has hardened, invert the pan so that the mold's upper half is touching the flames.

9. Spread 1 tablespoon of batter around the mould using the pastry brush, then repeat the process on the other side.

10. Spread 120 grammes of anko evenly in the middle of the mould and push down slightly to flatten any peaks. Add about 1 heaping spoonful of the mixture.

11. Add a heaping spoonful of batter and swirl it around with the pastry brush to cover.

12. Turn the pan over as soon as you close and secure the lid. Give it two minutes to cook. Then, after 2 minutes on one side, turn the pan over and continue cooking.

13. Remove the cover and examine the hue. You may keep cooking it until it becomes golden brown and crisp if it seems to be still rather light. If the Taiyaki becomes stuck in the pan, you can loosen it by heating the side that's touching the burner and prying it out with a toothpick or skewer.

Anmitsu Recipe

PREP: 15 min, TOTAL: 30 min, SERVINGS: 2

INGREDIENTS

- ½ tablespoon agar agar
- 1 cup sugar
- ½ tablespoon lemon juice
- 3 cup water
- ¼ cup bean paste
- 1 Numbers orange
- 1 Numbers cherry

INSTRUCTIONS

1. To make the jelly, soak agar agar in one cup of water in a dish for about one hour. Now, add one cup of water and the drained agar agar to a pan set over low heat. After cooking over low heat, stir in 1/4 cup sugar and 1/4 tablespoon lemon juice. Whisk the liquid while heating the mixture to a boil over low heat. Allow the mixture to thoroughly combine by simmering for a few minutes. Take off the heat source and let aside to cool. It will solidify into a jelly once chilled.

2. To make the syrup, heat up another pan to a medium temperature and combine half a cup of sugar and one cup of water. Cook this mixture over medium-low heat until it thickens. Re-simmer until the liquid takes on the viscosity of syrup by adding the remaining lemon juice.

3. Slice the orange and cut the pieces of jelly to serve. Place them in a basin and garnish with cherries or other desired fruits. To enjoy, drizzle the sugar syrup and sweet bean paste over!

Mizu Yokan Recipe

PREP: 1hr 0 min, TOTAL: 1 hr 15 min, SERVINGS: 4

INGREDIENTS

- 1 stick dried kanten
- Water for soaking kanten
- 1 ¼ cup water
- 1 cup brown sugar
- ¾ pound/1 1/2 cup anko

INSTRUCTIONS

1. Assemble the components.

2. Get the mixture of gelatin ready: Soak the dried kanten (agar agar) stick in water for one hour, or until it becomes soft, in a big dish.

3. Take the kanten out of the water and squeeze the water out of the softened kanten.

4. Tear the kanten into little pieces using your hands.

5. Place the kanten pieces or kanten powder in a medium pan with 1 1/4 cups water. Stir continuously and bring to a boil. Reduce the heat to a minimum. Simmer for the kanten to fully dissolve. Remember to constantly swirl the water and kanten.

6. Add the sugar and thoroughly whisk.

7. Include readymade koshian or ankhor delicious red bean paste. Make sure the bean paste is diluted in the agar agar and water combination by stirring continuously. Simmer the mixture for a longer time until it thickens. Take off the heat.

8. Transfer the mixture into a plastic container that is rectangular and shallow. After letting it cool to room temperature, put it in the refrigerator to keep it cold. The mizu yokan ought to solidify.

9. Serve the cold mizu yokan after cutting it into tiny blocks.

Mitarashi Dango (Japanese Rice Dumplings with Sweet Soy Glaze)

PREP: See recipe, TOTAL: See Recipe, SERVINGS: See Recipe

INGREDIENTS

- ½ cups plus 3 Tbsp. joshinko flour
- ½ cups plus 1 Tbsp shiratamako flour
- ½ tsp. sugar
- 4 to 5 skewers
- ¼ cups sugar
- 3 tbsp. mirin

- 3 tbsp. soy sauce

- 1 tbsp. potato starch or cornstarch

- ¼ cups plus 2 Tbsp. water

INSTRUCTIONS

1. To bring water to a boil, pour it into a pot of medium size and bring it to a boil. Place a medium-sized dish of cold water next to the burner.

2. Combine the sugar, shiratamako flour, and joshinko flour in a large basin. With a wooden spoon or your hands, gradually mix in ½ cup cold water until a dough begins to form. The dough should be kneaded by hand until it is smooth. Next, using a tiny cookie scoop or measuring spoon, divide the dough into fifteen sections the size of a tablespoon. Finally, roll each component into a smooth ball using the palms of your hands.

3. Drop the dango balls into the boiling water and give them a gentle swirl to prevent them from adhering to the pot's bottom and to one another. Simmer for 10 minutes, or until the dumplings float to the top, and then cook for an additional minute.

4. Move the dango balls to the cold water using a slotted spoon or spider skimmer, then let them chill for three minutes. Once again draining the dango balls, thread them onto five 6–7-inch skewers, with three balls each skewer. The skewers should be placed on a small platter and left alone.

5. In a small saucepan, mix together the starch from potatoes, sugar, soy sauce, mirin, and half a cup plus two tablespoons of cold water to produce the glaze. Stirring continuously, bring the mixture to a thick glaze by cooking it over medium heat for about 5 minutes. After removing the dango balls from the fire, quickly coat them with the glaze and serve immediately.

How to Make Matcha

PREP: 5 min, TOTAL: 5 min, SERVINGS: 1

INGREDIENTS

- ¼ teaspoon matcha

- 2 ounces hot water, 175°F is ideal

- 6 ounces additional hot water or steamed milk of choice, almond milk, oat milk, coconut milk, dairy milk, etc.

- Maple syrup, honey, or other sweetener, optional

INSTRUCTIONS

1. Toss the matcha to remove any lumps and place it in a cup or small dish.

2. Add the two ounces of heated water. Beat quickly from side to side with a matcha whisk or tiny conventional whisk until the matcha is completely distributed and forms a frothy layer on top.

3. Continue whisking until frothy after adding the remaining 6 ounces of hot water or steaming milk. If desired, sweeten to taste with honey, maple syrup, or your favourite sweetener.

Amazake

PREP: 10 min, TOTAL: 10 hr 10 min, SERVINGS: 5

INGREDIENTS

For the Non-Alcohol Amazake with Rice Koji:

- ¾ cup uncooked Japanese short-grain white rice
- water (for cooking the rice porridge)
- 1 cup water
- 1 cup rice koji

For the Low-Alcohol Amazake with Sake Lees:

- 4 cups water
- ½ cup sake lees
- ¼ cup sugar
- 1 pinch Diamond Crystal kosher salt (to taste)

INSTRUCTIONS

To Cook Amazake with Rice Koji:

1. Compile all of the components. Place ¾ cup of uncooked Japanese short-grain white rice in the pot of a rice cooker after rinsing and draining it. Fill the cup with water to the brink of the porridge. Add water to the ordinary white rice 4 cup line if there isn't a porridge water line. Press Start after choosing the Porridge option on your rice cooker, or follow the directions on the rice cooker to prepare the porridge.

2. The porridge should be around 175°F (79°C) after it is ready. Remove the rice cooker's inner pot containing the porridge.

3. Gradually stir in 1 cup of water to the porridge, ⅛ cup at a time, and mix well after each addition. Using an instant-read thermometer, ascertain the porridge's temperature. Since koji mould cannot survive beyond 140°F (60°C), the temperature must drop to that level.

4. Crush the cereal and stir in 1 cup of rice koji when it gets 140°F (60°C). To combine, give it a good stir. To ensure that the rice koji and porridge are well soaked, make sure there is enough water to cover them. If not, keep it at 140°F (60°C) by adding warm water.

Reinstall the inner pot into the rice cooker. 5. After selecting the Keep Warm (or Extended Keep Warm) option, cover the rice cooker's opening with a towel. To prevent the rice cooker from overheating, keep the lid completely open. Simmer the mixture for 8 to 10 hours, monitoring the temperature every hour for the first three hours and stirring once and again. At all times, make sure the temperature maintains between 125°F and 140°F (50–60°C).

6. After 8 hours, a pleasant aroma will begin to emanate from the combination. When the mixture is cooked through, it should smell sweet. After turning off the rice cooker, place the inner pot in a large basin of cold water to halt the cooking process and allow it to cool. Once the Amazake has cooled down, move it to a large sterile container.

To Assist:

Remove the necessary amount, dilute with hot or cold water to your desired consistency (I like mine thicker and undiluted), and serve warm (reheated) or cold. Reheat the Amazake to moderate temperature to preserve the living enzyme. If heated beyond 140°F (60°C), the koji enzyme will perish. If you'd like, you may add grated ginger. Smoothies with avocado, banana, and soy milk are a hit with my kids.

How to Prepare Amazake Using Sake Lees (Sake Kasu):

1. Compile all of the components. Tear up ½ cup of sake lees, also known as sake kasu.

2. In a big saucepan, bring 4 cups water to a boil. Dissolve the sake lees in the water using a mesh strainer. It is recommended to soften the lees in the water first so they will dissolve more readily, albeit this procedure may take some time. There should be no pieces remaining in your amazake.

3. After it has dissolved, stir in ¼ cup sugar and a pinch of kosher salt Diamond Crystal. Allow to decrease and simmer until desired consistency is reached. About fifteen minutes is how long I cook and decrease the amazake since I want a little thicker consistency. Warm or hot, serve, and enjoy!

To Keep:

1. Store in the freezer for up to one month or in the fridge for up to one week.

Ochazuke (Japanese Green Tea Over Rice)

PREP: See recipe, TOTAL: See Recipe, SERVINGS: See Recipe

INGREDIENTS

- 1 cup (130 g) hulled white or black sesame seeds

- 6 ounces (170 g) salmon or smoked salmon fillet

- Sea salt

- Freshly ground black pepper

- 1 tsp. vegetable oil

- 2 cups (350 g) cooked white rice
- 3 cups (710 ml) hot freshly brewed green tea
- 2 Tbsp. Surigoma or a combination of nori and toasted sesame seeds
- 2 Tbsp. thinly sliced scallions, white and light green parts
- 1 Tbsp. grated fresh wasabi or wasabi paste (optional)

INSTRUCTIONS

1. A medium dry skillet should be heated at medium-low heat. until the seeds are aromatic and faintly coloured but not browned. Sesame seeds will get aromatic but will not change colour. Once a few seeds sprout, it's time to start keeping a close eye on them and removing them from the heat. Once the seeds are toasty, transfer them to a mortar and use a pestle to smash them to the appropriate consistency (you can also use a food processor). For a pleasing texture, leave some seeds intact. The seeds may be kept for up to a month in the refrigerator or another cold, dark area if they are totally cooled and stored in an airtight container.

2. Set the grill to high. Spread the oil over an aluminium foil-lined baking sheet. Salt and pepper the fish before cooking. Season the fish with salt and pepper. Finish the salmon to your liking by broiling it for 6 to 10 minutes after placing it on a baking sheet. The meat will flake after cooling.

3. Spoon the flaked salmon over each individual rice dish after dividing the rice among them. Over each, at the table, ladle approximately 1 cup (240 ml) of the hot tea and sprinkle with the sesame seeds, scallions, and surigoma or nori. If desired, garnish the dish with wasabi.

How To Make Kombu Tsukudani (Simmered Kelp)

PREP: 40 min, TOTAL: 1 hr 0 min, SERVINGS: 4

INGREDIENTS
- 20 g Dried Kelp

- 2 Liters Water
- 50 ml Tamari Soy Sauce
- 2 tsp Mirin
- 2 tsp Sake
- 1 Tbsp White Sugar
- ½ Tbsp Rice Vinegar
- 1 tsp Sesame Seeds (Optional)

INSTRUCTIONS

1. Combine all of the ingredients.

2. Transfer the kombu to a big pot, cover with two litres of water, and leave for half an hour. Remove the kelp and slowly heat the mixture until it reaches a boil. To use the kombu dashi in other Japanese meals, keep it! Note: Use whatever kombu you have left over from preparing dashi and continue with the recipe's remaining instructions.

3. Slice the kombu into thin strips after cutting it in half. A good tip is to use a sharp knife and a firm grip while slicing the kombu since it might be slippery.

4. Put the sliced kombu, sake, mirin, sugar, and tamari soy sauce in a small saucepan. After bringing to a boil, simmer the mixture until all of the liquid has reduced.

5. If preferred, add Japanese Sansho pepper or sesame seeds. Savour it as a side dish with sake or over rice!

Cabbage Asazuke (Quick Pickles)

PREP: 5 min, TOTAL: 5 min, SERVINGS: 10

INGREDIENTS

- 560 grams napa cabbage
- 90 grams carrots
- 30 grams scallions
- 5 grams ginger

- 20 grams salt
- 2-3 chili peppers
- 5 grams konbu

INSTRUCTIONS

1. Weigh the veggies if you are using a different quantity, and then multiply that amount by.3. This will indicate how much salt to add. For instance, we're using 685 grammes of veggies in total for our meal, and 20 grammes of salt is equal to 3% of 685 grammes.

2. Combine all the ingredients and place them into a large zippered bag.

3. Seal the bag after eliminating any remaining air. Place the sack inside one tray and cover it with a smaller tray that has cans weighted on it.

4. When the cabbage is transparent and has released a lot of liquid, the asazuke is ready to consume.

Shiso Furikake (Rice Seasoning)

PREP: 5 min, TOTAL: 45 min, SERVINGS: 3

INGREDIENTS

- 1 cup loosely packed fresh perilla leaves I used green perilla here
- 1 ½ tsp toasted sesame seeds
- ½ tsp salt
- ½ tsp sugar
- ½ tsp gochugaru ,optional

INSTRUCTIONS

1. Trim the shiso leaves of their stems, then spread them out evenly in a layer on a baking sheet. For approximately 40 minutes, or when the leaves are quite dry, dry them at 170°F (75°C).

2. Take off the burner and place the leaves in a mixing dish. Crush the leaves into tiny flakes using your hands. Don't go overboard. If not, you'll be left with a powder.

3. Include the sugar, salt, gochugaru (if using), and toasted sesame seeds. Mix well and pour into a small jar or other container.

4. Sprinkle for a delicate nutty and herbal flavour over cooked white rice, tofu, or veggies! Furikake may be kept at room temperature in an airtight container for up to two months.

Buta no Square simmered

PREP: 5 min, TOTAL: 2 hr 15 min, SERVINGS: 3

INGREDIENTS

- 600 grams skinless pork belly
- 45 grams fresh ginger
- 12 grams garlic
- 6 grams niboshi
- ⅓ cup sake
- 1 ½ cups water

- 1 tablespoon granulated sugar
- 1 tablespoon soy sauce
- 1 teaspoon salt

INSTRUCTIONS

1. Cut the meat into squares that are 25/50.

2. Place the pork belly, fat side down, in a small, just big enough pot with a heavy bottom (like a dutch oven) so that the pork is contained in a single layer. Heat the saucepan to medium-high and let the pork alone until the fat side is golden brown.

3. Place each piece on a platter after turning it over to brown the other side.

4. Add the garlic, ginger, and niboshi and cook until fragrant and browned.

5. Include the sake and bring it to a boil until the alcohol is gone.

6. Return the pork to the saucepan and stir in the sugar, soy sauce, water, and salt. After bringing to a simmer, reduce the heat, and cover tightly with a lid.

7. Simmer for approximately two hours, or until the pork belly is falling apart tender.

8. Strain the braising liquid and skim off any excess fat if serving the square simmered immediately. However, it's better to leave this in the refrigerator for the

whole night since this allows the meat to absorb more flavour and will also make trimming the extra fat much simpler.

9. Reheat the pork belly slightly before serving. Cut into slices and present with part of the cooking liquid, spicy mustard, and steaming greens.

Japanese Egg Sandwich (Tamago Sando)

PREP: 5 min, TOTAL: 15 min, SERVINGS: 2

INGREDIENTS

- 6 large eggs

- ¼ cup Kewpie mayonnaise

- 2 teaspoon milk

- ½ teaspoon sugar
- ½ teaspoon salt
- ⅛ teaspoon pepper
- 2 green onion diced
- 4 slices milk bread
- 2 tablespoon butter room temperature for spreading

INSTRUCTIONS

1. Hard boil the eggs. To boil, add half of the water to a medium saucepan. Carefully use a slotted spoon or spider strainer to transfer the eggs to the boiling water. Over medium heat, gently simmer the eggs for nine minutes. Make an ice bath.
2. Leave the eggs to cool and peel them. After 9 minutes, use a slotted spoon or spider strainer to extract the eggs, and then drop them into an ice bath to chill for a minimum of 5 minutes. After the eggs have cooled, carefully remove their shells.
3. Break the egg yolks apart. Before dicing the egg whites, cut the eggs in half lengthwise. Remove the yolks.
4. Gently combine the egg salad ingredients. An egg yolk, kewpie mayonnaise, milk, sugar, salt, and pepper should be whisked together in a small bowl until they are completely smooth. Add the sugar and add the salt and pepper. Then, gently incorporate the green onion and chopped whites.
5. Put together the egg salad sandwich for Japan. The egg salad should be spread on top of each slice of bread after it has been spread with butter. Place the second slice on top and gently push down. If you'd rather not, you may cut the crusts in half and trim them.

Hamachi Kama (Yellowtail Collar)

PREP: 5 min, TOTAL: 15 min, SERVINGS: 2

INGREDIENTS

- 2 hamachi or kanpachi collars
- 1 tbsp mirin
- ½ tsp kosher or sea salt
- lemon wedges
- soy sauce

- yuzu ponzu

INSTRUCTIONS

1. Position the oven rack six to eight inches below the oven's top. Select the high setting (500°F) for the grill.

2. Cover an aluminium foil baking sheet.

3. Place the fish skin side down on the sheet, then lightly coat each collar with kosher or sea salt and brush with mirin.

4. After setting the baking sheet on the oven shelf, broil it for seven to ten minutes. The fish will have flaky, delicate flesh and a gently browned, blistered appearance. View the reference photographs above.

The fish should be plated and served with lemon wedges and yuzu ponzu or soy sauce for dipping. Enjoy the fish after adding some lemon juice.

Tamago Kake Gohan (Egg Over Rice)

PREP: See recipe, TOTAL: See Recipe, SERVINGS: 1

INGREDIENTS

- 1 cup hot, cooked white rice
- 1 raw pasteurized large egg
- ½ teaspoon soy sauce or tamari
- ½ teaspoon mirin
- Pinch kosher salt
- Pinch hondashi
- Pinch Aji-no-moto MSG powder (optional)

- 1 raw pasteurized large egg yolk (optional)

TOPPING OPTIONS:

- Furikake
- Bonito flakes
- Sliced scallions
- Pickled ginger

INSTRUCTIONS

1. Pour 1 cup of white rice onto a serving dish. Make sure it's scorching hot. Create a small depression in the middle with chopsticks or a fork. Place one raw egg into the depression. If you want it very spicy, add half a teaspoon of soy sauce or tamari, half a teaspoon of mirin, a sprinkle of kosher salt, a pinch of hondashi, and a bit of MSG powder. (On the other hand, you may combine the egg and spices in a another dish, whisk them together, and then pour them over the rice.)

2. To integrate the egg into the rice, whip the mixture rapidly with chopsticks or a fork until it turns pale yellow, creamy, and somewhat foamy. Adjust the spices to your liking by tasting. If desired, garnish with one raw egg yolk. Depending on your preference, you may garnish with furikake, bonito flakes, scallions, or pickled ginger. Instantaneous service is required.

Home-Style Tamagoyaki (Japanese Rolled Omelette)

PREP: 5 min, TOTAL: 15 min, SERVINGS: 4

INGREDIENTS

- 2 large eggs

- 1 ½ tablespoons (20ml) homemade dashi or hondashi , or more or less as desired (see note)

- 1 teaspoon (5ml) usukuchi soy sauce, plus more for drizzling

- 1 teaspoon (5ml) mirin

- An oil-soaked paper towel, folded up into a small bundle, for greasing the pan

- Grated daikon radish, for serving

INSTRUCTIONS

1. Use chopsticks to thoroughly mix the eggs in a small bowl, being sure to remove any visible whites. Whisk in the soy sauce, mirin, and cooled dashi.
2. You want the pan to be hot enough that the eggs will softly bubble and sizzle when they contact it, but not so hot that they brown quickly. Preheat the tamagoyaki pan over medium-high heat until you can feel moderate heat radiating off of it when your hand is held an inch or two from the surface. While the pan is heating, hold the oiled paper towel between two chopsticks and lightly cover the whole surface, being sure to get into all the crevices. You may keep the oiled towel in a small dish close by.
3. Once you've added a quarter of the egg mixture, turn the pan so that the eggs uniformly cover the bottom. Any big bubbles that pop may be easily punctured with your chopsticks.
4. Start rolling the egg when it's completely set on the bottom but slightly damp on top: Take the pan off of the hob and slide one chopstick under the topmost layer of eggs. Using a rapid upward motion of the pan, carefully raise and roll the egg sheet until it comes halfway to the handle. Keep going until the egg sheet is completely rolled up and near the handle. The egg sheet is very floppy, making this layer the most challenging to roll. However, if you find that you are having problems, just use your chopsticks to press the sheet, gathering it at the handle end.
5. Preheat the pan again. Grease the region next to the handle after sliding the omelette roll to the other side of the pan, then rub the greased cloth all over the exposed surface of the pan (the centre and far side).
6. Transfer one-third of the egg mixture left in the pan and equally distribute it over the bottom of the pan, creating four layers. To expose the raw egg behind the curled piece, use your chopsticks to pull it up. Keep cooking, popping any big bubbles that burst, until the top of the next layer is somewhat dry and just set.

7. Once again, roll the fried egg log towards the handle, this time inserting a chopstick under the far edge and flopping it over as you go. To complete the egg, repeat the stacking and rolling procedure twice more.

8. If using a bamboo sushi mat, carefully transfer the wrapped tamagoyaki to it. Roll it up firmly but gently to ensure a consistent shape; lay aside for 3 minutes. Serve the tamagoyaki on a platter, cut it in half if you want, and top it with a little mound of grated daikon radish. If you like, you may pour a little more usukuchi soy sauce on top of the daikon.

Natto (Japanese Fermented Soybeans)

PREP: 12hr 0 min, TOTAL: 12 hr 0 min, SERVINGS: 4

INGREDIENTS

- 2 cups dried soybeans (10 1/2 ounces; 300g)
- Half of 1/8 teaspoon natto starter spores, such as Nattomoto

INSTRUCTIONS

1. In a big saucepan, add the dried beans. Put the beans in a bowl of water and let them soak for eight to twelve hours, or until soft.

2. When Using a Stovetop Cooktop: Give the soaked beans a good rinsing and put them back in the saucepan. Boil beans in a pot of fresh water, being sure to cover them by at least an inch. The beans should be cooked until they are soft

but not mushy, which should take about four hours (see notes), reducing heat to a constant simmer. At the same time, sterilise a big heatproof mixing bowl by pouring boiling water into it, making sure the water covers most of the inside surface, and then pouring it out. After the beans have been drained, add them to the big mixing basin. Get rid of the cooking liquid.

3. Make care to rinse the soaked beans well in three changes of fresh water if you're using a pressure cooker. Add a minimum of one inch of fresh water to the beans. Lock the top of the pressure cooker. Preheat the pressure cooker to high and cook for 10 minutes. Let the pressure go out of your body as it will. For instructions on how to boil beans till tender but not mushy, see the notes. At the same time, sterilise a big heatproof mixing bowl by pouring boiling water into it, making sure the water covers most of the inside surface, and then pouring it out. After the beans have been drained, add them to the big mixing basin. Get rid of the cooking liquid.

4. At the same time, sterilise the utensils by boiling them in water for 5 minutes with a small metal bowl, a stainless steel soup spoon, and a teaspoon. Once sterilised, move the utensils to a clean surface. To prepare the containers for fermenting the soybeans, fill them with boiling water and then pour the water out. To activate the natto starter spores, combine them with 1 tablespoon of

water in a sterile small basin using a sterile teaspoon. Add the mixture to the boiling soybeans right away. Toss the soybeans with the sterilised soup spoon to combine them well and spread the starter evenly.

5. Separate the beans into clean, large, airtight containers, ensuring that each one has a layer of beans no deeper than 2 cm. Use the lid to secure the cheesecloth cover.

6. Place the containers in a warm area to guarantee that your beans are maintained at a temperature of around 100°F (38°C). This may be achieved in a yoghurt maker, a proofing drawer, or even an off-gas oven with the oven light turned on. See notes for more on what to do if your soybeans don't look and smell like this; let stand for 20 to 24 hours, When the beans smell cheesy and nutty and are completely coated in a thin white coating, they are done. Rotate the containers every 12 hours and inspect them every hour beginning around the 20th hour.

7. Put the containers in the refrigerator and let the beans ferment for another 12 hours. It is now time to enjoy the natto.

Tsukemono-Nukazuke rice bran pickle

PREP: 10 min, TOTAL: 240 hr 10 min, SERVINGS: 1

INGREDIENTS

- 800 ml Water
- 800 g Roasted Rice Bran
- 80 g salt
- 250 g matured rice bran mixture Optional
- 2 inch Kelp (5cm)
- 1 dried chili
- 6-8 outer leaves cabbage for maturing the rice bran bed

INSTRUCTIONS

1. After boiling the water to get rid of chlorine, let it cool down.
2. In the same container you use for pickling, add the roasted rice bran.
3. Toss the toasted rice bran with the salt and stir to combine.

4. Once the water has cooled, pour it into the container and stir it well using your hands.

5. Fill up the rice bran bed all the way with the garlic, chilli, and konbu kelp.

6. To prevent the formation of further germs, flatten the top surface with your hands, wipe the container clean, and then cover it.

7. Allow to overnight in the fridge.

8. Remove the container from the refrigerator the next morning. Gently place the cabbage leaves into the nukadoko, a pickling bed made of rice bran, and cover them completely with rice bran.

9. To clean the interior of the container, use damp rags to wipe it down.

10. Let it sit at room temperature for the night with the lid on. *5

11. After the cabbage leaves have been removed, mix the rice bran bed well the next day.

12. Scatter more rice bran on top, top with another cabbage leaf, press down to level the surface, and then use damp towels to wash out any excess.

13. To let the rice bran pickling bed grow, repeat steps 2–4 three or four times instead of one.

14. If you want to pickle the rice bran bed, you need to repeat the previous steps three or four times.

15. Before you start to pickle, wash and prepare the veggies you want to use. *3

Miso Soup with Steamed Rice

PREP: 5 min, TOTAL: 10 min, SERVINGS: 4

INGREDIENTS

- 4 cups Dashi
- ½ carrot
- ¼ onion
- 2 green onions
- 1 cup steamed rice
- 4 Tbsp miso paste

INSTRUCTIONS

1. Dashi packets may be used to make dashi broth. Alternatively, you are free to use any Dashi that follows our Dashi formula.
2. Carrots should be cut into matchsticks. Onion, finely slice. Finely chop the green onion. While Dashi is heating, sauté the onion and carrot for 2 minutes. After that, cook the steamed rice for one more minute.
3. Add the miso paste and stir until all of the paste is dissolved. Add a green onion garnish just before serving.

THE END

Printed in Dunstable, United Kingdom